Manufacturing the News

Manufacturing the News

by Mark Fishman

University of Texas Press
Austin and London

The publication of this book was assisted by a grant from the Andrew W. Mellon Foundation.

Library of Congress Cataloging in Publication Data

Fishman, Mark, 1947–
 Manufacturing the news.
 Bibliography: p.
 Includes index.
 1. Reporters and reporting. I. Title.
PN4781.F5   070.4   79-22374
ISBN 0-292-75054-4

Requests for permission to reproduce material from this book should be sent to Permissions, University of Texas Press, Box 7819, Austin, Texas 78712.

To Alex and Doris Fishman

Contents

Acknowledgments

An undertaking of this size would not have been possible without the help of several people. Three deserve special attention.

Pamela Fishman saw me through this project, assisting me in concrete ways from the earliest mumblings and grumblings about news to the proofreading of this book. She offered so many insights into the workings of the media that I can no longer distinguish her ideas from mine.

D. Lawrence Wieder generously provided a complete set of field-notes from his research on the same news organization I later studied. These materials gave my analysis a depth it otherwise would not have had. More than anyone else, Larry Wieder helped me see newswork in a fresh light and, at the same time, showed me what good ethnography looks like.

Harvey Molotch was one of the main inspirations for this study when it began as my doctoral thesis in sociology. His suggestion that I first try my hand at journalism before observing reporters from a distance proved wise indeed. His criticism of earlier drafts broadened my analysis in ways that ultimately strengthened it. But most importantly, his energy and enthusiasm reminded me that it was all worthwhile.

In addition, I wish to acknowledge the valuable comments and helpful suggestions of Gaye Tuchman, Thomas Wilson, and Don Zimmerman.

Finally, I wish to thank Drew Humphries, Linda Marks, Florence Tager, and Susan Wolf—all members of the Park Slope Work Group—whose relentless editorial and conceptual criticisms made this work more readable. As a result, I hope, one does not have to be a sociologist to read this book.

Manufacturing the News

1. News and Public Events

Sociologists and journalists are in the same business. They both produce social facts. But the methods and the character of their findings usually differ. This book focuses on the character of social facts that journalists produce every day and the methods they employ to generate them. My purposes are not to evaluate newsworkers' methods and findings against social scientific criteria of objectivity and adequate methodology. Instead, I want to explain how what we read in newspapers today is constructed, how it gets there.

How a society comes to know itself is a matter that receives little attention in the social sciences. Yet one of the things in greatest abundance in any society are accounts produced within the society about itself. People not only do things, they constantly make accounts of what they do. Interoffice memos, neighborhood gossip, income tax returns, social scientific theories, opinion polls, atlases, personnel files, political speeches, book reviews, courtroom transcripts, car repair manuals, business inventories, newspaper articles—all are "stories" people tell each other about their world for purposes specific to the society: to describe social mobility, to explain the collapse of a government, to predict rain, to instruct auto mechanics, to propagandize voters, to collect taxes, and to sell books.

The issue of how a society knows itself might be just another interesting question if societal accounts were incidental to the functioning of society, but they are not. As W. I. Thomas (1928: 582) noted, our picture of how the world works is integrally tied to how we work in the world. By acting in accordance with our conception of the way things are we concertedly make them the way they are, whether we are treating pieces of paper as money, conducting a routine conversation, or electing a new president. Thus, money is good for exchange only because people treat it that way and enforce this treatment on one another: that things can be otherwise becomes evident during inflationary panics.

To call this a "self-fulfilling prophecy" (Merton 1968: 475–490) is to trivialize what is in fact an essential feature of social life. Rather than an aberration, the construction of social reality is inherent in the very nature of interaction. Not only is the social world known to its members through their accounts of it to one another, but these accounts are part of the very social world they describe and make intelligible. As a consequence, accounts of the world receive their meaning and are intelligible only in relation to their context (Garfinkel 1967; Wieder 1974; Zimmerman and Pollner 1970). The social construction of reality is endemic and unavoidable and, thus, cannot be set aside as a special event occurring in peculiar circumstances.

In this study I am concerned with the process by which a very special and important reality is socially constructed: the public reality of mass media news. The news media appear to play a significant role in the construction of large-scale social phenomena, from mental illness (Scheff 1966: 69–80; Nunnally 1961) to crime (Steffens 1931; Davis 1952; Roshier 1973; Jones 1976). Yet little systematic study, least of all empirical research, has been undertaken in this regard: how are mass media news accounts actually produced, and how are they produced so that they create and recreate the social phenomena they report?

As a way of introducing the reality construction perspective of this study, the history of a crime wave is presented in some detail.[1] If we want to understand public events, this case will show why we must look to the specific means by which a community knows of their existence. That is, we must examine the news production process.

Assembling a Crime Wave

In late 1976 New York City experienced a major crime wave. For seven weeks all the city's media were filled with reports of brutal crimes against elderly citizens. Perhaps the most important consequence of the crime wave was that it publicly formulated a new category of crime, with typical victims (poor elderly whites who had not fled neighborhoods in transition) and typical offenders (black and Hispanic youths with long juvenile records).

The public outcry against these crimes was almost immediate. The mayor of New York vowed to make the streets safe for the elderly. He denounced the juvenile justice system and allocated more manpower to a special police squad focusing on elderly victimization (the Senior Citizens Robbery Unit). Bills were introduced in the state legislature to increase punishment for violent juvenile offenders. Community meetings were held on the problem. Months later, a nationwide Harris poll showed that fear of this new kind of crime was widespread.[2]

During the crime wave I was inside a New York City television newsroom observing the work routines of an assignment editor who selected news and assigned reporters and camera crews to stories. My research began to focus more and more on the coverage of crimes against the elderly as I noticed aspects of newswork that seemed to be contributing to the existence of the crime wave. In the course of these observations, I discovered something that made me wonder whether the entire news production process was *creating* the crime wave it was reporting. A reporter who had been researching a feature story on crimes against the elderly told me he had found that police statistics showed a *decrease* in these crimes compared with the previous year. The reporter was puzzled and eventually decided to ignore the police figures. He felt they were unreliable and incomplete, and anyway he had to do the story as originally planned because the whole issue was too big to pass up or play down.[3]

As I checked with other journalists, I found that many had doubts about the reality of the crime wave. Still, no one could resist reporting it. The crime wave was a force weighing heavily on their judgments of what was news, and it simply could not be ignored. Clearly some kind of system was operating. Something in the news production process was creating the crime wave. What was it?

My observations in the television newsroom indicated that a crime wave is little more than a theme in crime (e.g., crime against the elderly, crime in the subways) that is heavily and continuously reported. Crime themes, like any theme in the news (e.g., the truckers' strike, the war in Northern Ireland), are organizing concepts. They allow one to see diverse incidents as related insofar as they can be seen as instances of some encompassing theme. News themes allow editors to organize an otherwise confusing array of events into packages or groups of interrelated news items.

For instance, one evening's program at the TV station during the crime wave began with three stories about crimes against the elderly:

1. Police apprehend three young muggers of an elderly Queens couple.
2. Senior citizens meet with police at a Queens precinct to discuss fighting crime.
3. How the Senior Citizens Robbery Unit operates.
These were followed by three stories about youth crime:
4. Guns and drugs are seized from gangs in the Bronx.
5. Two gang members are arrested in a knife-point robbery.
6. An ROTC cadet is charged in the stabbing death of another cadet. The program continued with a few stories about the police department and then broke for a commercial.

Themes give news shows and newspapers a presentational order. Individual occurrences can be grouped together as instances of a theme, and these thematic groups can be placed near each other when they are seen to share common elements. For example, the stories on crimes against the elderly and on youth crime were both about youthful offenders and what the police are doing about them.

But journalists do not use news themes simply to give an audience the appearance of order. Editors need themes to sort through and to select a few stories from the masses of copy they receive each day. To understand how this works, let us see how the assignment editor put together the beginning of the news show just described.

The assignment editor did not begin his day knowing that crimes against the elderly would receive top billing. When he started work at 8:45 AM he already knew of two stories he would most likely cover.[4] One was a pretaped report on the Senior Citizens Robbery Unit (SCRU) fighting crimes against the elderly. This feature, which eventually ran as the third story in the evening newscast, was part of a continuing series the station had been airing. The second was a feature story on a "food fair" going on that afternoon in Manhattan. The editor planned to send a reporter and camera crew to this, but before he did he wanted to line up, as he put it, "some better stories" for the day.

The assignment editor's first hour of work was devoted to scanning his various sources of news in search of lead stories. He sifted through reams of wire service news, read the press releases mailed to the station, scanned the police dispatches of the last night's criminal incidents, and looked to other media for story ideas. He read the *Daily News* and *New York Times* and intermittently listened to an all-news radio station.

In the *Daily News* he found a small story on how laid-off firemen and subway police might be rehired. He thought this would be a good story because "this indicates things may be turning around in the city." In other words, the editor saw the relevance of the item by perceiving it as part of a current newsworthy theme (New York's fiscal crisis).

Still, he despaired that he had no real news, that this was a slow news day. But at 10 AM two things happened. First, when scanning the police crime dispatches, the editor found that an elderly couple had just been mugged in the 113th precinct in Queens. As he was clipping this he heard over the all-news radio that the 112th precinct in Queens was going to hold a crime prevention meeting with senior citizens. He now knew what the beginning of his newscast would be and what he had to do:

1. He would send a reporter to the 113th precinct to get on film whatever he could about the mugging.

2. Then the reporter could go to the nearby 112th precinct to cover the police meeting with the elderly.

3. These reports would be followed by the pretaped feature on SCRU.

4. The story on the rehiring of firemen and transit police, as well as whatever else on crime came in that day, would all follow the three lead stories in some as yet undetermined order. The story on the food fair would be placed further back in the show.

Notice that each story on the elderly seen independently might not have merited attention. Seen together, however, all of them were made newsworthy by the perception of a common theme. The "discovery" of the theme of crime against the elderly made the day's news come together; in fact, this was really a rediscovery of a theme that for some time had been in the news.

Our assignment editor was not alone in his practice of closely following the news of his competitors. All journalists depend on other news organizations for their sense of "what's news today."[5] This means that news judgments can spread quickly through time and space. Morning papers provide story ideas to editors of afternoon papers and evening broadcasts. Afternoon and evening media provide a sense of the latest developments for the morning media. Because these news organizations may be in different cities and regions, news judgments can spread throughout an indefinite expanse of territory.

As journalists notice each other reporting the same news theme, it becomes established within a community of media organizations. Journalists who are not yet reporting a theme learn to use it by watching their competition. And when journalists who first report a theme see others beginning to use it, they feel their original news judgment is confirmed. Within the space of a week a crime theme can become so "hot," so entrenched in a community of news organizations, that even journalists skeptical of the crime wave cannot ignore reporting each new incident that comes along. Crime waves have a life of their own.

It is tempting to conclude that crime waves are the result of some dynamic contained within a community of interacting news organizations. But this is not the whole story. After all, how do crime waves first arise? And why do only a few crime themes ever swell into crime waves?

No matter how much journalists expect to see a certain theme in the news they cannot continue to cover it without a steady supply of fresh incidents to report as instances of a theme. Therefore, we must look at the sources of crime news to understand the origin and continued existence of crime waves. At the television station I studied, these sources were exclusively law enforcement agencies. All news organizations who cover crime routinely rely on the police for their knowledge of crime (Chibnall 1975: 51–52; Sherizen 1978: 210–213). The main channel through which our assignment editor and his colleagues throughout the city first knew of crime was a teletype in the newsroom (called the police wire) which carried about a dozen crime dispatches a day from police headquarters. Once the crime wave was underway, the police wire was quite important in sustaining coverage of it. But how did the wave begin?

The crime wave can be traced back to October 24, 1976, when a series of feature articles on crimes against the elderly appeared in the New York *Daily News*. The reporter who wrote this series told me that he received considerable help from SCRU, a newly formed police squad specializing in robberies and assaults on the elderly. On October 7 the reporter first wrote a story on two crimes with elderly victims which had appeared on the police wire on the same day. At that time an editor thought it would be a good idea to do a series of feature stories on this kind of crime. Other news organizations had done such features in the past.

While researching these stories, the reporter was in frequent contact with SCRU. The police unit let him know they felt beleaguered, understaffed, and that they were fighting a battle that deserved more attention. After he finished the feature stories, the reporter was able to follow up the series with several reports of specific incidents because SCRU officers were calling him whenever they knew of the mugging or murder of an elderly person. This kept the issue alive in the *Daily News*, and soon the theme began to catch on in other news organizations.

One incident in particular brought all the city's media into covering the theme. Police from SCRU, in a phone conversation with the *Daily News* reporter, complained that the courts were releasing juvenile offenders almost as fast as they were apprehended. The reporter replied that to write about this problem he needed to know of a specific incident. The police told him about a recent case of a black youth who was released on $500 bail after being charged with beating and robbing an 82-year-old white woman. This story was published. Upon reading it in the *News*, a state legislator (who sat on a juvenile justice subcommittee) got access to the youth's record of prior offenses and found that one of these was a homicide. The legislator telephoned several of the city's media, who then publicized this latest development. Seeing the kind of coverage his case was receiving, the youth promptly jumped bail. That event quickly made headlines throughout the city. At this point, the mayor called a press conference and "declared war" on crimes against the elderly. This too was heavily covered in all media.

One element of the mayor's battle plan was the expansion of SCRU and its plainclothes operations. This probably increased the number of offenses the police knew about and thus could report to the press. Moreover, the war on crime included the creation of a new accounting procedure inside the police department which suddenly made a large number of fairly common occurrences visible to the press. In effect, police in precincts were ordered to consider victimizations of the elderly as "unusual incidents" to be reported directly to headquarters, which, in turn, was to transmit these to the media via the police wire. (Before this order only the most bizarre or brutal incidents were considered unusual enough to tell headquarters about.) Thus, a week and a half after the coverage started, the police wire was steadily supplying the press with fresh incidents almost every day. And when there was an occasional lack of crimes, there was plenty of activity among police, politicians, and community leaders to cover.

However, the police policy of closely monitoring and reporting crimes against the elderly was only designed for a three-month period. About the time that the special monitoring stopped, coverage died down and the crime wave was over.

Creating Public Events

New York's crime wave was a public event produced through newswork. How do we mean this? In what sense can we say that the crime wave was a construction of reality? Let us answer this by taking up a question we are inclined to ask about this crime wave and, indeed, about anything the media portrays to a public. Is it real? We might first want to say that the crime wave was a distortion of reality, but let us consider the matter more carefully.

If we think of crime waves as nothing more than waves of media coverage (leaving open the question of whether or not they are related to anything happening on the streets), then New York's crime wave was certainly real. As a wave of publicity, it focused public attention on a new issue and formulated that issue at the same time. The media were both the means by which anyone in New York "knew" about the crime wave and the means by which the crime wave was assembled. News organizations created the wave, not in the sense that they invented crimes, but in the sense that they gave a determinant form and content to all the incidents they reported. Out of newswork arose a phenomenon transcending the individual happenings which were its constituent parts. A crime wave is a "thing" in public consciousness which organizes people's perception of an aspect of their community. It was this "thing" that the media created.

The crime wave was also real in another sense. News organizes our perception of a world outside our firsthand experience. But in doing so, the media are not simply putting certain images in people's heads. The media construct something in the society as well as in people's heads. Even though one cannot be mugged by a crime wave, one can be frightened. And on the basis of this fear, one can put more police on the streets, enact new laws, and move away to the suburbs. Crime waves may be "things of the mind," but they are real in their consequences.

Moreover, the consequences of news are not simply byproducts of the newsmaking process. They are integral to it. At the beginning of the crime wave we saw how the increasing news coverage affected the unfolding of events and how these unfolding events led to the escalation of coverage. Once underway, we saw how the wave of publicity seemed to be generating itself. Recall the three stories on crimes against the elderly that the TV assignment editor found to lead off his program. One was about an actual crime. The other two (the community meeting and the feature report on SCRU) were both consequences of the wave of coverage already in existence. Yet both stories contributed to the further existence of the wave. At least in part, news creates the environment it reports. The consequence of news is more news.

Thus, crime waves are public events not only visible through newswork but to a significant extent produced within it. Even so, can't we say that the coverage of "crimes against the elderly" reflected some real crime situation in New York? The wave of media coverage provided the appearance of a crime spree in 1976. Was this real? There is no simple answer.

On the one hand, it would be absurd to suggest that there really was no problem for New York's elderly in 1976. In several areas of the city, old people were living in a state of fear. They knew from firsthand experience and from word of mouth that the situation was bad. The Senior Citizens Robbery Unit concurred and took it upon themselves to bring the issue to light when the opportunity arose.

On the other hand, if we try to grasp some larger picture of crime in the city, we fail to find evidence of a crime spree around the time of the media coverage. If we rely on the city's crime statistics, we could conclude that there was not an increase in victimization of the elderly.[6] But the city's official crime rates are not reliable indicators of actual amounts of crime.[7] We cannot answer the question with the available data.

We might be able to resolve the issue if we had better data gathered by the best social scientific methods available. Let us say that we did our own victimization survey for the period in question. If our hypothetical survey showed consistently decreasing rates of victimization of the elderly, then we might say that news distorts reality. If our survey showed consistently increasing rates, then we might say that news reflects reality. But news organizations did not first know the real situation and then distort or reflect it through the newsmaking process. At the time of the wave of publicity, no one knew exactly how much crime was happening on the streets. Whether victimization was increasing or decreasing was irrelevant to the methods journalists used to detect crime and assemble the crime wave. For a wave of publicity to have existed there need only have been *some* incidents on the streets and considerable concern about them among those sources the media relied upon.

If we wish to understand the public event that New York experienced or, indeed, any public event portrayed through news, then we must examine the actual methods journalists use to construct reality. It is not useful to think of news as either distorting or reflecting reality, because "realities" are made and news is part of the system that makes them.

Phenomena like crime waves are neither "media hype" nor "pseudo-events" (Boorstin 1961). Neither are they what we might know them to be were there no mass media. What is out there already, before its becoming a public event, is up for grabs (Molotch and Lester 1974). Public events have never been known apart from the institutionalized means of communication which formulate those events in society. In our age, these institutionalized means of communication are the mass media. They set the conditions for our experience of the world outside the spheres of interaction within which we live. If we wish to know how we come to see the public sphere the way we do, then we must ask how the media transform an indeterminant world into a formulated set of events. In other words, we must study journalists' routine methods for producing news.

Studying Newswork

The earliest approaches to the study of news characterized news-work as an information processing system, the most important function of which was selecting events for the news. Studies of journalists as "gatekeepers" tried to isolate the variables which determined how editors selected written news copy (White 1964; Gieber 1956, 1964; Warner 1970) and how reporters chose what to write about (Carter 1958; Gieber 1960; Gieber and Johnson 1961). Studies of journalists as "organization men" tried to identify the organizational forces which subverted the professional ideal of objectivity by causing reporters to omit information and slant what they wrote (Breed 1955; Stark 1962; Matejko 1970; Warner 1971; Sigelman 1973). In all these studies, how journalists wrote anything at all, how they formulated what they saw and heard, was not a topic of interest.[8] The news production process was conceived of only as a news selection process.

This is because most researchers assumed that news either reflects or distorts reality and that reality consists of facts and events out there which exist independently of how newsworkers think of them and treat them in the news production process. The unquestioning acceptance of these assumptions led traditional media researchers to identify their central question as: how does the news organization and the individual gatekeeper select what will pass through the channel into print? Thus the central concern of traditional media studies has been the *selectivity of news*.

The central concern of this book is the *creation of news*. By using the reality construction perspective I ask: how do newsworkers make news? To answer this I focus on the most fundamental elements of newsmaking: the *work routines* with which journalists approach—to use William James's phrase—a "buzzing, blooming world of particulars," and the *methods* by which they transform that world into news stories.

I hesitate to use a phrase like "the creation of news" because of its pejorative connotations and because it suggests the fabrication of news out of whole cloth. Both senses are misunderstandings of my interest in the creation of news. Newsworkers are faced with a reality in their work: they meet somebody saying something. How they construe that somebody and that something into news is neither totally arbitrary (out of whole cloth) nor totally fixed by the nature of what they confront.

Knowledge is not a passive record of perceptions; it is the consequence of something people do. The knower interacts with the world and in the process gives the world both a determinant form and content. The interaction here is not simply a mental operation; it involves social interaction, and it is a form of work.[9]

News is a determinant form of knowledge not because the world out there already comes in determinant forms but because people employ specific methods which strive to organize that world into something coherent. News is the result of the methods newsworkers employ. Were different methods used, different forms of news would result and publics would know the world outside their direct experience in a very different way.

The perspective of this study takes journalists' routine work methods as the crucial factor which determines how newsworkers construe the world of activities they confront. The journalist's relationship to the world he or she covers is not a direct one but is mediated by practical concerns: how to report a world of activities within the constraints of publication deadlines and news space limitations, how to determine the factual character of accounts, how to formulate events into a story, and so on. To do this, newsworkers do not invent new methods of reporting the world on every occasion they confront it. They employ methods that have been used in the past; they rely upon the standard operating procedures of their news organization and of their profession.

Therefore, as a methodological strategy I will begin with the view that the routine work methods of journalists are capable of explaining the distinct character of media news—and not that such things as contrived news leaks, publicity stunts, the suppression of stories by editors, or the planting of stories by interested parties are primarily responsible for the quality of news reports. My point is *not* that the latter practices are of little consequence or do not exist. I am

simply arguing for the need to study and understand the consequences of routine newswork before assessing the role of other influences in the newsmaking process.

I am distinguishing here between two levels of newsmaking. The
first and most fundamental level is that of routine journalism, where-
in the daily methods and standard practices of journalists give rise
to routine news. By routine news I mean the standard fare that fills
newspapers day after day: not the shoddiest or the most exceptional
pieces of journalism, but what most newsworkers would consider
good, plain, solid, honest, professional news reporting. The second
level of newsmaking, what might be termed manipulated journalism,
involves the moves and countermoves in a political game in which
news is treated solely for its instrumental value in the service of particular interests. This is another kind of work that can go on in the
newsmaking process. New York's crime wave clearly involved news
sources who had a stake in the crime issue. They strategically used
their power to make news in order to formulate what was going on
in ways that were compatible with their interests (Molotch and Lester 1973 and 1974).

Manipulated journalism presupposes routine journalism: it is
built on a foundation of routine news practices which it attempts to
direct. In New York, the mayor, the state legislator, and the Senior
Citizens Robbery Unit were able to promote successfully their versions of what was happening and what could be done about it. But
their ability to do so depended on the routine practices of journalists
—practices which tied newsworkers to these sources and which led
newsworkers to treat their sources' accounts not as versions of reality but as "the facts."

Both routine journalism and manipulated journalism need to be
studied. We must first understand routine newsmaking so that we
can determine what the work methods of journalists are capable of
producing without external contrived interference. We then will be
in a better position to assess the extent and effects of second level
phenomena in the news production process.

Because this study does not begin by picking out items from newspapers and analyzing their properties, I need no initial criteria of
what constitutes news. Rather, my method is just the opposite: my
concern with routine journalism means I will begin by examining

the daily work of journalists in order to describe and analyze a process in which something gets produced, oriented to, and called "news." The nature of news for me is from the outset an open question, something this study aims to illuminate.

The Organization of This Book

The news production process can be dealt with in four analytically separate stages, consisting of the methods by which newsworkers (1) detect occurrences, (2) interpret them as meaningful events, (3) investigate their factual character, and (4) assemble them into stories. My presentation and analysis of newswork is organized in terms of these four stages.

The first stage, news detection, is dealt with in Chapter 2. There I will describe the task structure of reporting work, both inside and outside the newsroom: what are the everyday constraints on journalists who are workers in an organized enterprise which publishes and distributes newspapers? Examining the overall structure of work routines—including both the interrelationships of reporting tasks and the environment of constraints which defines it—means examining the news "beat." As will be shown, the complex pattern of work routines that make up the beat constitutes a "coverage structure" which determines what reporters can be exposed to in the first place. Thus, we will see how the beat defines the world of possible news.

The next three chapters explain how, through the use of specific methods, the world of possible news is progressively narrowed into the world of actual news. Taken together, one could say that Chapters 2 through 5 describe a process by which newsworthiness is determined.

Chapter 3 deals with the first aspect of how the world of possible news becomes actual news: by what means do journalists *interpret* what they see, hear, and read? This amounts to asking how a mere occurrence can be seen as a public event (Molotch and Lester 1973, 1974), or, alternatively, how reporters make sense of and see relevance in what they are exposed to. The issue of interpretation turns out to be critical because much of what goes on under the reporter's nose is ignored, and ignored in a systematic way. In Chapter 3, particular attention is given to those incidents which are not noticed ("nonevents"), since why reporters fail to pay attention to them clarifies the nature of routine news judgments. They show how a reporter's nose for news is closely tied to a local sense of occurrence, i.e., definitions of the situation imposed by others who are part of the social settings which the beat reporter frequents.

Chapters 4 and 5 raise the issue of how reporters investigate potential news events. Chapter 4 delves into journalists' grounds for investigation: when and why do newsworkers decide to proceed (or not proceed) to further investigative work on events that have already been detected and interpreted? The question amounts to asking: what are the journalistic methods of verification and standards for "facts"? If something is seen initially as a "plain fact," it is judged simultaneously not to require further investigative work. Thus, Chapter 4 reveals the meaning of the journalist's distinction between plain facts and matters of speculation, opinion, etc. This distinction is important because I am not assuming that anything in itself is a plain fact. Rather, I want to know how "fact" is socially produced. Chapter 4 shows how and why newsworkers can invest the character of plain fact in certain things, while other matters, if they are to become publishable news, necessitate more effort on the reporter's part.

Chapter 5 examines what reporters do with matters that require further investigation. I am concerned here with specific methods of news investigation and formulation: how do journalists know where to look to undertake such an investigation, how do they weigh evidence, and how do they organize their efforts so that investigative methods lead directly into a formulated story? In this chapter I sketch out how newsworkers notice inconsistencies, errors, and suspicious happenings; what leads them to see the most interesting facets of a case; and, finally, how they act on these definitions of the emerging story.

In the sixth and concluding chapter, I draw out the implications —especially the political implications—of my findings. I discuss the way in which a free and uncensored press consisting of independent news organizations winds up providing a uniform view of the world which can only be characterized as ideological. The roots of this ideological hegemony are traced to the routines of news detection, interpretation, investigation, and assembly. Ultimately, the origins of news ideology are traced to the practicalities of newswork imposed by the existing structure of news organizations in this society.

The Research Setting

The analysis of news reporting presented in the next five chapters is based on extensive participant observation of newswork on a single newspaper in California, the Purissima *Record*.[10] Because the focus of this study is the production of news, the data presented are based primarily on observations of staff reporters and their supervisor, the city editor. I have not included in this study a description and analysis of the work of editors at the news desk assembling written stories into the newspaper. On the Purissima *Record*, the core of the news production process occurred at the level of reporters' work where news was detected, investigated, and formulated. My observations at the news desk showed that it was rare for news stories produced by staff reporters to be cut or changed by editors in this last stage of the process.

At the time of the study (1973–1974), the Purissima *Record* held a virtual monopoly over news consumption in both the city of Purissima (population 75,000) and its metropolitan environs (population 150,000). The paper's daily circulation of 45,000 approximated the number of households in the metropolitan area. No other daily paper read in the community came close to this kind of distribution.

Moreover, the *Record* maintained by far the largest news producing organization with the most extensive coverage of various aspects of the community. Its news department consisted of 37 full-time reporters, editors, and photographers—at least four times the news gathering resources of any other media in the area (one television station, two radio stations, and one weekly "alternative" newspaper).

The *Record*, as well as the smaller news organizations, covered the community by following activities in city hall, county government, and the police department. Only the *Record* extended its coverage beyond these agencies into the court system, educational institutions, suburban governmental units, environmental protection agencies, and the financial, small business, and real estate communities. Furthermore, while other media covered local government and law enforcement agencies, the *Record*'s reporting was considered more comprehensive. Its reporters attended meetings more regularly and followed the doings of secondary commissions, committees, and boards that other media learned about only second-hand, usually by reading the *Record*. For these reasons, the *Record* was generally acknowledged as Purissima's "newspaper of record." Many of the area's residents saw it as Purissima's only local news medium.

As with all case studies, the generality of my findings can be questioned. I believe, however, that the news organization chosen for study is fairly typical of American newspapers in terms of its internal structure, monopoly over the local news market, and position in the community. Most importantly, the routine news practices I found on this newspaper closely correspond with journalists' practices mentioned by a variety of independent sources: biographies, autobiographies, and other reports by journalists, as well as empirical studies of news practices on other newspapers.[11]

At various points in this study, where important differences in news routines exist in other media organizations, I discuss the meaning of the differences. It remains an open question just how general my findings are with respect to news produced through other forms of mass media (notably television and radio) and news produced outside American society.

Purissima's Press Corps

It was primarily in city council meetings and, to a lesser extent, at county board of supervisors meetings that reporters from Purissima's news media were regularly in each other's presence covering the same events. During these meetings they formed a small press corps. There were five reporters at city hall (representing the *Record*, the alternative weekly newspaper, the TV station, and the two radio stations) and three reporters at county government (representing the *Record*, the alternative paper, and the TV station). These small groups sat at a press table where they watched the meetings, took notes, and talked with each other. During breaks and lulls in the meetings, they would leave the table to talk with news sources, get coffee, or just gossip among themselves. Relations among these journalists were quite friendly, with no overt signs of hostility or competition.

In April 1973 my field observations began in these two press corps settings. I wanted to do several months of participant observation of the routine work practices of *Record* reporters in these settings and, later, in other settings including the *Record* newsroom. But I needed some grounds on which to relate to newsworkers other than as a researcher. At the time I felt that my status as a sociologist might have gotten me a few interviews with journalists, but it would not have allowed me a longterm, closeup view of their work. So I began working for the Purissima *Voice* (the alternative weekly newspaper) as their city hall and county government reporter. As a novice reporter I would have both continuing and easier access to the routine workings of the press. For seven months, until January 1974, I wrote a weekly news column about the meetings of the city council and county board of supervisors.

Within three weeks of my first appearance at the city and county meetings, I was treated by reporters and other regulars as a familiar fixture at the press table. I was immediately on a first name basis with all the reporters, and soon conversation was easy. For the first two months most of this talk centered around the immediate environment of the meetings: who was who in the governmental agencies, how things worked in the bureaucracies, what was happening in the meeting, what was likely to happen next, and so on.

As long as I was not interrupting their work, I could seek, and would freely get, considerable advice and information on the operations of local governmental agencies, the meaning of the ongoing activities in the meetings, and whom to talk to about any given issue. During the many breaks and lulls in the meetings when the reporters could talk with each other without interruption, I was able to ask most of these questions. During these periods I also learned a great deal about the not-so-public side of local government through the considerable gossiping the reporters did with each other. As a novice, these reporters taught me all the "basics" I needed to know in order to report competently on city and county government. As time wore on, however, I found that I was learning more about how local government operated than about how reporters worked.

For all their initial friendliness and help, I ran into real problems when I tried to probe into the details of newswork. I could see reporters taking notes during the meetings, but what were they thinking? To ask them would have been to interrupt their work, and I was brushed away the first few times I tried this. I watched, and sometimes heard, reporters talking with news sources, but it was awkward to tag along behind them and downright suspicious to take notes of their interviews. Most frustrating of all were my unsuccessful attempts to question journalists about how they covered, or were going to cover, a specific story. After a few questions I would be met with polite rebuffs or excuses to end the conversation. I learned not to question reporters directly about their practices, but to wait patiently and let this come out in the course of a conversation about something else.

Eventually I realized why I was having these troubles at the same time that I was getting so much friendly help. That is, I learned the ways of the press corps. My general impression of friendliness in press corps relationships was based on a number of specific cooperative arrangements between reporters. These arrangements not only aided reporters in doing their work, but they also made for an overall pleasant atmosphere at the press table and fostered a general sense of solidarity among reporters. For example:

Updating. If a reporter arrived at a meeting after it began, or if a reporter stepped out for a brief period, they could then ask any other journalist who was present to bring them up to date on what they had missed. Each journalist was expected to fill in any other journalist.

Incidental information. Reporters felt free to ask and frequently did ask each other such details as the correct spelling of a name, the identification of a person present at a meeting, clarification of bureaucratic procedures, and the like.

Referral. If journalists were unable to answer a colleague's question, not only would they say so but they would also refer the colleague to someone who could be expected to know the answer.

Global leads. Reporters would tell colleagues where and when possibly important news events were to take place, e.g., a press conference or an official meeting. That is, they would alert each other to a setting in which news might be found, but they would not hand over specific newsworthy material per se.

Gossip. Reporters exchanged considerable quantities of gossip relevant to the topics they reported: the private lives of local news-makers, the behind-the-scenes activities on various issues, private feuds underlying public debates, and so on. Without explicitly trying to assist each other, this gossip in fact kept each reporter filled in on what "really" was happening and what was likely to happen with events they wrote about. This kind of information had to arise in the natural course of conversation. If any reporter appeared too eager to find out the details of some case, the discussion would be politely ended or its topic changed. Often the eager reporter would be referred to a proper (official) source, or given a global lead where the reporter might find out what she or he wanted to know. Gossip also would become guarded whenever it was seen as touching on too many details of some story presently being reported by a journalist.

As the reporters' rules of gossip indicate, within the press corps there are also proscribed practices enforced by cordial sanctioning. These taboos are what underlay the mistakes I made whenever I tried to question journalists about their work. Reporters generally referred to these prohibitions under the label of pumping: they all have something to do with requests for too much help, too much newsworthy information. For example:

Free tips. Directly asking a colleague for specific tips and leads to news stories was prohibited. Without asking for it reporters could be, and sometimes were, tipped to specific news stories by colleagues. But they could never rely on other reporters as sources of tips and leads because the information could not be requested.

Free stories. A reporter was prohibited from asking a colleague for specific information about newsworthy happenings that the reporter had not covered in person. For members of the press corps, this was equivalent to a reporter's asking a colleague to do his or her work.

Divulging sources. It was definitely taboo for a reporter to ask other reporters to identify their news sources.

As these do's and don't's demonstrate, reporters will help each other out in "small ways." They will not exchange news stories per se, although they will exchange gossip. They will not tip each other off to specific stories, although they will give each other global leads to stories. They assist each other as long as it is clear each is already doing her or his own work. On occasions, they will "scoop" one another on stories, with no hard feelings expected or permissible. But competition for news in Purissima was not fierce. Scooping and being scooped were not daily concerns for reporters.

Methodology I: Observations as an Apprentice

My seven months of experience as a novice reporter provided invaluable data that no newsworker could have told me. What was taken for granted by experienced reporters and what I learned firsthand was the background knowledge one had to know in the first place to determine "what's going on" in a setting in order to "see" news in it. In short, I was learning what it took to report news competently, and I knew this at the time. My field notes from this period were, in part, a kind of diary reflecting not only what I saw of the work of other reporters but also my observations of myself learning to report news.

A number of phenomena reported in this study developed out of these observations of my apprenticeship. My early field notes were filled with particular things in the meetings I did not understand. These were matters I felt I had to know about in order to write news stories and which made me turn to more experienced reporters for help. My ignorance alerted me to the specific kinds of information journalists used to determine what's going on, enabling them to sort out trivial from important matters. This led to my formulation of journalistic schemes of interpretation and schemes of relevance in Chapter 3. The schemes I discuss there are ones I saw myself having to learn and use in order to translate a confusing array of governmental activities into meaningful written news stories.

Similarly, my apprenticeship field notes reflected how I learned to pay attention to things happening at meetings. I learned when to take breaks and time-outs from long sessions by noticing what other reporters were and were not paying attention to. Most importantly,

I discovered why certain occurrences were not of interest and, thus, why they became invisible to reporters. These parts of my field notes led to the formulation of nonevents in Chapter 3.

Several months into the apprenticeship phase of my field work I began to recognize the nature of my difficulties in finding out more details of how *Record* reporters operated. I began to change my identity from journalist to sociologist. I told the *Record*'s city and county reporters that I was not only a reporter for the *Voice* but also a sociologist doing research on how news gets made. They seemed interested in helping me and agreed to be interviewed at length about their work. As a sociologist, I found it easier to get answers to more of my questions about reporters' actual practices.

Methodology II: Observations as a Researcher

After seven months of participant observation as a reporter, I stopped working for the *Voice* and went into the *Record* news organization for a closer look at how reporters and editors produce news. There I observed interactions between the city editor and staff reporters. I followed two reporters (the county government and police court beat reporters) through their work days. I watched how all three editions of the newspaper were assembled at the news desk by editors. And I interviewed various reporters and editors in depth. Before I discuss these field methods, I must describe another source of data which was available to me at the end of my apprenticeship.

From August 1964 to January 1965, D. L. Wieder did extensive participant observation of reporters on the Purissima *Record*. Wieder gave me access to these data (over four hundred pages of field notes) before I began my own observations at the *Record*. His five months of research provided observations of the same type I was planning to make on the same news organizations ten years later. Wieder recorded the everyday work practices of reporters and editors by following them through several work days. Besides observing the assembly of the newspaper at the editorial desk for eight work days, he recorded eleven days of work on the police court beat and six days of a general assignment reporter's work.

Wieder's field notes were helpful in several ways.[12] I began reading and analyzing his observations during the period I was working as an apprentice reporter. They provided a wealth of data beyond what I was already collecting. While I had been observing the city hall and county government reporters in the same settings week after week, Wieder's notes showed reporters' work in other settings doing a variety of tasks, in some cases over three and four consecutive days.

This material not only underscored my need to do similar observations, but it broadened my understanding of what I was already observing. By placing the work methods of reporters in the larger context of an entire day's or week's work, and in the context of the operations of the *Record*'s editorial department, I started to develop what appears in Chapter 2 as the two systems of constraints within which beat reporters operate. Moreover, the analytic comments Wieder inserted in his notes, in combination with what I gleaned from scattered observations throughout his notes and my own, allowed me to identify several key phenomena in newswork even before I began interviewing reporters and following them through their work days. For example, the reporter's round discussed in Chapter 2 was plainly visible and partially analyzed in Wieder's field notes, as were some of the principles of determining fact which are discussed in Chapter 4.

The use of Wieder's notes at that point in my research had its advantages and disadvantages. I knew at the time that reading his notes would affect my own future observations. I was priming myself to look for certain phenomena in newswork that Wieder had seen. This meant that I could not safely use his findings to confirm independently my own research.

However, reading and analyzing Wieder's field notes before the second phase of my observations proved to be quite advantageous. I was able to concentrate my time and efforts strategically when I went into the *Record* news organization. In effect, in a shorter period of observation I could zero in on certain phenomena only partially documented in Wieder's notes. I could spend less time and effort on other phenomena already well documented in his observations. For example, because Wieder had already done the groundwork, it took me very little time to confirm the existence of the round on each of the beats I observed. Instead, I focused my efforts on getting detailed records of other areas of the news production process: the

nature of the talk between reporters and their city editor and between reporters and their sources; what reporters did at the point
they condensed information from some original account into their
own notes for a story; and what reporters did at the point they began
to plan out and write news stories.

After seven months of working as a reporter and after having
read five months' worth of Wieder's observations, I was thoroughly
familiar with the field setting I was about to enter (or reenter). It
did not take several days of observation at the *Record* to acquaint
myself with the observational field.

Therefore, for relatively short periods between February and July
1974 I observed the routine practices of journalists by following
them through a total of nine work days: two days on the news desk,
three days on the police court beat, and four days on the county
government beat. Whenever possible, I tape-recorded reporters' talk
with editors and news sources, and I taped intermittent interviews
with them before and after they undertook routine tasks. Finally, I
conducted in-depth interviews with four journalists: the city hall
reporter, the county government reporter, the police court reporter,
and the city editor. These interviews were conducted both before
and after observations of their work.

In all, the findings presented in this study are based on data which
cover over six hundred hours observing six different reporters on the
same news organization over two periods: 1964–1965 and 1973–
1974.

2. Exposure to the Newsworld

The Beat

In this society the most widely recognized function of newspapers is to report news, to report happenings in the world. There are many conceivable ways one could organize a group of individuals to do this, but for at least the past one hundred years American newspapers have settled on one predominant mode of coverage known as "the beat."[1] As a matter of fact, the beat system of news coverage is so widespread among established newspapers that *not* using beats is a distinctive feature of being an experimental, alternative, or underground newspaper.[2]

Ever since its establishment in the 1920s the Purissima *Record* depended heavily on beats to cover local news. By the time of the present study, the *Record*'s editorial department was thoroughly organized around a system of beats. Over two-thirds of the *Record*'s reporting manpower was devoted to covering some fourteen different beats, from the city hall beat to the nature beat.

Reporters who do not generate news from a beat work on what is called general assignment. They are stationed in the newsroom, and either the city editor (the immediate boss of the local reporting staff) assigns them stories to research and write or they suggest their own stories and get clearance from the city editor. In contrast, reporters working a beat are rarely assigned stories. They are expected to generate news from their beat on their own initiative. Routinely they spend more time stationed at their beat locations than in the newsroom. In comparison with general assignment reporters, beat reporters work autonomously. Removed from the city editor's direct supervision most of the day, the beat reporter is largely responsible for deciding what to cover and how to cover it. The purpose of the next four chapters is to explicate that responsibility, i.e., what it means to cover a beat and to generate news out of that beat. Toward that end we will see how potentially newsworthy occurrences are detected, interpreted, investigated, and formulated as publishable stories.

Although I have been speaking as if it were perfectly obvious what a beat is, in fact it is rather difficult to define and clearly distinguish beats from other phenomena of newswork. The beat is a journalist's concept, grounded in the actual working world of reporters. As such I can never absolutely distinguish a beat from, for example, an area of expertise that an individual reporter brings to the job and uses in writing stories. Nevertheless, from observations of work on what the *Record*'s reporters recognized as beats, I can outline several key concepts that clarify what a beat is and what makes beat reporting a distinctive system for covering news.

1. A beat has a history in the news organization that outlives the organizational histories of the individuals who work the beat. The *Record*'s city hall beat was covered by four different reporters in the past decade, but as an organizational structure for news coverage the city hall beat is perceived as substantially the same beat.

2. Superiors assign reporters to their beats. The reporter is responsible for, and has jurisdiction over, covering the beat. But the reporter does not own that beat. Insofar as the person is a reporter, the beat is theirs to be covered. Insofar as a reporter is anything else (a single woman, a grandfather, a gourmet), it is inappropriate to use that beat in connection with those other identities.[3] The beat is an office in Weber's sense (1947: 330–332).

3. The beat is a complex *object of reporting* consisting of a domain of activities occurring outside the newsroom. This object, this domain of activities, is coherent. The coherence of a beat simply means that a beat consists of something more than random assortments of activities. The people who produce the activities occurring within a beat territory, and the reporter who covers them, see these actions as sensibly connected in specific ways. Take the police beat, for example. One day the desk sergeant tells the police reporter that a prostitution ring has been busted; another day the reporter sees an arrest report concerning a prostitution case; another day he sees in the court calendar a preliminary hearing for a prostitution case, and so on. These occurrences are all connected: they comprise the judicial career of the same prostitution case. The police and the courts produce these connections; the reporter sees them.

Moreover, sequences of activities themselves are related to other sequences. Beat reporters, and others, see the relations among sequences in two ways. These turn out to be two alternative ways of defining the beat as an object of coverage. First of all, a beat reporter sees that a number of sequences of activities are all part of the same topic. For example, the police reporter not only perceives a single criminal case underlying and connecting all its various appearances, but the reporter also sees it topically, e.g., as a case of prostitution or as an instance of "the recent crackdown on victimless crime." Connected activities form topics which arise again and again within the beat. Over time, these topics define the beat.

Second, reporters see sequences of activities as related because they occur in the same physical locations, they are enacted by the same people, and they are subject to the same standard operating procedures. Here the beat is territorially defined, as a situated entity with stable locations, stable actors, and stable actions.

The topical and territorial ways of defining the beat represent a genuine duality in the journalist's concept of the beat. This distinction is apparent in the two ways newsworkers talk about their beats: as places to go and people to see or as a series of topics one is responsible for covering.

This duality is even more striking in the phenomenon of overlapping beats. In fact, it makes such overlapping possible. Both Wieder and I observed several cases where two beat reporters' jurisdictions for coverage coincided on the same specific news story, suddenly making it legitimate to ask something that had never needed to be asked: who should cover it? This happened whenever a topic associated with one beat moved into the territory of another beat.

To cite one example, the Nopal Valley beat reporter had been covering the issue of annexing Nopal to the city of Purissima for the preceding three years. One day the issue was coming up before the weekly meeting of the county board of supervisors, which is part of the territory of the county government beat. The Nopal reporter had topical jurisdiction; the county reporter had territorial jurisdiction. The reporters involved had to decide who should cover the story. The beat-as-a-territory and the beat-as-a-set-of-topics offered equally good grounds for claiming jurisdiction. The actual decision of who should do the coverage was always made on other grounds ad hoc, as each ambiguous case arose.[4]

The overlap of beats, while not unusual, is not a matter of constant attention among reporters. Journalists see the social world as so organized that topics and territories tend to coincide, i.e., there are stable locations in which certain topics stably reside. The newspaper's system of beats relies upon this perceived order to organize its coverage of the world. At the same time, the newspaper's system of beats helps sustain this view of social organization in American society.

4. The beat is a *social setting* to which the reporter belongs. The reporter becomes part of the network of social relations which is the beat. Within this network the reporter makes friends and enemies, passes gossip and shares secrets, conducts business, and goofs off. Like everyone else inside the beat, the reporter has a niche: a desk, a typewriter, sometimes a mailbox, and even a coffee mug. But unlike other insiders, being an insider is expressly part of the reporter's job.

This adds an interesting twist to my preliminary picture of the beat. Even though the reporter takes the social setting of the beat as the object of reporting, reporters are part of that object. They participate in the activities that they report. Ethnomethodologically speaking, reporters and their beats are *reflexively* related. On the one hand, reporters inquire into the beat as a "subject" inquires into an "object." On the other hand, the very grounds upon which the reporter does an inquiry are from "within" the beat and hence are part of the activities that make the beat what it is. The consequences of this reflexivity for both the methods of beat coverage and the products of that work will be discussed later.

The Detection of Events

How are events detected? How does the reporter know where to look for potentially newsworthy happenings on the beat? For that matter, how does the reporter recognize something as an event in the first place?

These questions have rarely been asked about media news production. Past literature and research on newswork have been predicated upon a set of common sense assumptions that steered investigators away from the entire issue of event detection because the topic appeared to be uninteresting, obvious, or trivial. Examining these presuppositions of event detection is worthwhile not simply because they are so widely held, but also because they are plausible hypotheses worthy of empirical validation or invalidation. These presuppositions can be stated as five principles.

1. Events are assumed to be self-evident. Reporters come to know events in ways so obvious as to be trivial: events are immediately given in perception. This means that reporters have practically no methods at all for detecting events. Newsworkers simply put themselves in a position to be exposed to occurrences, and events "jump out" at them. Provided they are exposed to events directly (in person) or symbolically (through talking with a news source), reporters "just know" events for what they really are.

2. Events are assumed to exist independently of their knowers. Whether the event is known or unknown in no way affects its existence. Who it is that knows the event in no way affects what it really is. The event and its detection stand independently of one another.

3. The methods for detecting an event are assumed not to create, alter, or otherwise affect the event as it is discovered. Specifically, the object of the reporter's coverage is intransigent to however the journalist may discover it or whatever the journalist may think of it. The methods of detection do not affect the object of detection.

4. An event is assumed to occur logically and temporally before the detection of that event. First the event happens, and then the newsworker detects what has happened. To suggest that reporters might know what has happened before its happening, or simultaneously with its happening, would be to defy common sense or to accuse the journalist of creating events out of thin air (which is to say journalists are not detecting anything at all).[5]

This fourth assumption is quite important because if it were not valid, then the second and third assumptions would also be invalid. An event could no longer be assumed to exist independently of its detection if events could occur within the same process by which they were detected.

The next and fifth presupposition is a "master assumption," an assumption about the previous four.

5. All of the above presuppositions hold under the assumption that the newsworker or an informant is not venal, corrupt, biased, or otherwise a defective observer. Knowingly or unknowingly, defective

observers will filter, distort, or make up what they perceive, or they will fabricate events in the process of searching for them. The above presuppositions are only valid for professionally and socially competent, well-intentioned reporters.

This last principle is particularly interesting. It implies that anyone who even questions whether journalists detect events in the manner suggested by the first four principles is someone embarking on a criticism of reporters as venal, corrupt, biased, or defective. The fifth principle is a first line of defense against doubting the other four assumptions: inquiry toward the presuppositions is turned into a debate over the corruption and bias of the news media. This is a trap. It deflects a manageable inquiry into a controversy which has no end. (Is objectivity possible? Should fairness be the journalistic standard instead of objectivity? Are journalists doing the best job possible under the circumstances? Etc.)

I point out this characteristic of the fifth principle for two reasons. First, because the presuppositions of event detection are critically analyzed, it is likely that some readers will misinterpret my remarks as accusations of venality, corruption, and bias within the ranks of the news media. That is how the fifth principle works to deflect an inquiry of newswork into a debate over the moral quality of newsworkers. My intention is simply to uncover what journalists' actual methods of event detection are. Second, the set of principles I have outlined is an excellent example of an ideology. I mean ideology in the sense that Smith (1972) defines it, as a scheme for interpreting a factual domain which contains procedures for *not knowing* certain things. We have seen how the fifth principle can close off inquiry into the other four. It can blind us from very real forces at work in the media, namely, newsworkers' actual methods for detecting events. With this in mind, let us take the blinders off and examine how beat reporters actually find and recognize newsworthy occurrences.

Preconditions of Exposure to the Newsworld

The question of how reporters detect potentially newsworthy events contains two separate issues. The first is a matter of the reporter's exposure to activities, documents, and talk on the beat. Because journalists cannot detect something they are never aware of, it is necessary to look at how reporters systematically expose themselves to occurrences. The second issue concerns reporters' resources for interpreting that which they are exposed to. Many phenomena on the beat will be right under the reporter's nose, but they may not be noticed or the reporter may deem them unworthy of attention. Reporters' methods for interpreting or making sense out of their environment will predispose them to see some things as events and others as nonevents. Journalistic event detection depends on both methods of exposure and schemes for interpreting what are possible newsworthy occurrences in the first place. For the remainder of this chapter I will examine reporters' methods of exposure.

On any beat there are an infinite number of activities to which the reporter could potentially be exposed. Consider the Purissima *Record*'s justice beat which covered matters pertaining to criminal activity and law enforcement within and around Purissima. The beat territory conceivably encompassed:

—several thousand square miles containing 500,000 potential law-breakers;

—three law enforcement agencies: city police, county sheriffs, and an FBI office;

—four penal institutions: one federal penitentiary, one city jail, and two county jails;

—two juvenile facilities;

—two entire court systems (municipal and superior);

—an extensive drug subculture;

—a moderate size skid row area . . . and so on.

The unwieldy size of this territory is nothing unique to the justice beat. Both the city hall and county government beats encompassed far more boards, councils, departments, committees, community groups, and regulatory agencies than could ever be covered by a single human being in the course of an eight-hour work day.

How can individual reporters cover all this ground, and cover it on a routine basis under daily deadlines? Reporters strategically and systematically expose themselves to only a few sources of information within their beat territories. Built into the reporter's job is a complex work routine which, following Wieder, I shall term the "round." This round provides for much of the reporter's everyday exposure to the beat and forms the basic foundation from which all beat work proceeds.

To understand how and why the round is structured as it is, it is necessary to view it in the wider context of the reporter's work world. Newswork occurs within an environment of constraints originating from two sources: the news organization for which the reporter works and the newsworld toward which the reporter directs her or his coverage. First let us consider the constraints emanating from the reporter's home newspaper.

Because they are working members of their news organization, reporters are under an obligation to contribute written news toward the daily production of the newspaper. Specifically, the responsibility for covering a beat carries with it the obligation to write something every day about the beat. From the city editor's perspective, the whole point of the reporter's beat work is to produce written stories that fill the local pages of the newspaper. The city editor's work, and the work of other editors at the news desk, routinely depends on beat reporters' generating expectable quantities of fresh news copy every day according to fixed deadlines.

During the periods of observation of the Purissima *Record* both Wieder and I found that the reporter's obligation to produce news copy every day held for all beats.[6] Moreover, with rare exception, beat reporters consistently manage to fulfill this obligation. Neither Wieder nor I observed a reporter who had no news copy to show for a day's work. The city hall reporter, for example, could recall only two days out of his four years on the beat when he wrote nothing at all. On average, beat reporters turned in from two to six stories a day. The exact amounts of news space the reporter aimed to fill each day varied considerably and was worked out every morning in a conference with the city editor.

The obligation to produce news every day was so strong that even when both the city editor and the reporter agreed that nothing was happening on the beat, the reporter was still responsible for writing something about the beat. When the city editor mentioned that the city hall reporter was going to have nothing to cover one day, I asked if this meant that the reporter would produce no copy.

Oh no. No, no. He's got all kinds of stuff to write. It's a bottomless pit.

City government, county government are both a bottomless pit. He [the city hall reporter] never has time to write everything he might write. (Fishman interview 2-13-74, p. 5.)

On another occasion I questioned the city editor (CE) on the same issue:

MF: Would you raise your eyebrows at a reporter not turning in any copy in, say, two or three days?

CE: (laughing incredulously) Yeah, I sure would. I don't know which would be worse off, him or me.

MF: And if he said, "Look, there's just nothing happening."

CE: (laughing again) Well, you can always find something, you know. (Fishman field notes 2-19-74, p. 4.)

Remember that this is the reporter's boss speaking. In both instances he is making it clear that "nothing happening" on the beat is simply insufficient grounds for writing no stories. The city editor conceives of the beat as a bottomless pit of stories where one can always find something to write about, and he expects his reporters to view it likewise. News editors constantly need beat stories to fill the newspaper. The sense of how little or how much is happening is largely irrelevant to the normative requirement for reporters to produce these stories.

This obligation to produce fresh news copy every day has important consequences for the daily work routine of beat reporters in that, whatever they do during the day, they must schedule these activities around the daily production schedule of the news organization. The reporter's obligation to write is an obligation to write under deadlines not of the reporter's choosing. At the *Record* all local stories were expected to be turned in to the city editor around 12:30 PM but no later than 1:00 PM. No matter where reporters were or what they were doing on their beat, they had to allocate their time and arrange their schedules so that they could return to the newsroom to write their quota of stories in time. Their work day had to be arranged around the deadlines of the home news organization even though their coverage work was focused on a domain of activities that usually paid no heed to these deadlines.[7]

The constraints on the reporter originating from the newsworld are more difficult to characterize than the constraints of deadlines and story quotas emanating from the home newspaper. Unlike the news organization, the beat does not present itself as a single sphere of activities. Not only do different beats consist of very differently organized domains of activities (e.g., the justice beat consists of a system of criminal justice while the city hall beat consists of a system of municipal administration), but even the same beat contains within it very differently organized spheres of action (e.g., the justice beat encompasses both the operations of the police and the machinations of the courts).

It is a fundamental fact of beat work that the reporter must deal with a plurality of worlds of information (news sources in the broadest sense). Such sources differ as to where they are located; at what times they are available; by what means they may be tapped (by telephone, through personal inspection, by appointment with a spokesman, or through a clandestine informant); and whether the information sources can be expected to be cooperative or recalcitrant to the reporter's inquiry. Beat reporters who want to cover a heterogeneous collection of sources have to adapt their work routines to the varying opportunities of access with which they are presented. Thus, each beat requires very different coverage routines, different work rounds individually tailored to the particular activities within the beat's territory.

But there is more to be said about the way reporters' beat work is organized by the domain of activities that they cover. The availability of each source of information is predictable for the reporter because availability is itself a product of systematically organized work within various beat settings. A city hall which schedules its city council meetings, formalizes agendas of business, files its reports and communications, and keeps consistent office hours is a beat setting which makes sources of information predictably available to the reporter. To the extent that actors within various settings in the beat territory are engaged in orderly, concerted, systematic work, their activities follow a pace internal to the settings themselves. The same work logic internal to the setting that makes for the availability of information also produces the pace at which newsworthy occurrences unfold. In other words, whether reporters are tracking down information or observing something as it happens, their own coverage work is closely bound to the specific operating procedures and the particular paces of work endemic in the organizational settings on the round. The predictability of information and events for the reporter is systematically produced by the people within beat settings. This is so to the extent that those settings are bureaucratically organized. As we shall see, reporters' sources of information are found, in fact, within such highly organized settings.

In short, the reporter's own work routine must pay heed to two rather differently constituted spheres of activity. Covering a beat requires that the reporter follow bureaucratically organized activities and information which unfold at a pace independently of the time demands and writing limitations imposed on the reporter by the home news organization. Planning commissions cover agenda items, juries bring in verdicts, and rescue parties count the dead all in their own time. Beat reporters' need for news hinges on the amount of news space they are asked to fill and the deadlines within which they must fill it. These constraints are determined by considerations in the news organization having nothing to do with occurrences on the journalist's beat. The pace at which stories are assembled into a finished newspaper (assembly-time) and the pace at which events develop and information is made available to reporters (event-time) are organized on quite separate temporal dimensions.

Reporters' work falls within both these dimensions. They write stories under the constraints of assembly-time, while the activities and materials upon which these stories depend are made available under the constraints of event-time. Reporters must gear their activities to both spheres, and they must do so on a daily basis. This is precisely what the round accomplishes. It represents a particular method reporters employ for structuring their work as they routinely move in and out of each world of activities.

The Beat Round

The city hall, county government, and justice beat reporters all made highly regular, carefully scheduled rounds through specific sets of agencies and organizations on their beats. In addition to our direct observations of daily work on these three beats, interviews with other beat reporters and with the city editor indicate that some sort of routine round of activities is a central feature of all news beats on the Purissima *Record*.[8] To illustrate what a beat reporter's routine round of activities consists of, I shall describe in detail a single round—that of the *Record*'s justice reporter, Gene Slovekin. Here is what happened every working day on his police court beat.

Slovekin started his job when he arrived by car at the county sheriff's department at 7:30 AM. The first thing he did was to pick up from the watch officer's room a file box of the previous evening's arrest and investigation reports. He took these documents to a small office, a "press room," reserved for his use where there was a desk, telephone, and typewriter.[9] He systematically scanned each document for newsworthy arrests or investigations. In this file and all subsequent files at the sheriff's and police headquarters, the justice reporter was looking for two types of news: crime stories and crime briefs. Crime stories varied in length from about four to eighteen column inches and were located on the first or second page of the local news section. Crime briefs were very short reports, usually one sentence long, which appeared along with a variety of other miscellaneous briefs on a special page of the paper entitled "News and Notices in Brief." When the reporter encountered materials for a crime story, he took notes and later, when he returned to the newsroom, typed up a story from them. When he encountered materials for a crime brief, he typed up the short report from the document on the spot.

After searching through the arrest and investigation reports, Slovekin returned to the watch officer's post to look through a file of coroner's reports for any newsworthy deaths from the previous evening. Then, returning to his small office, the reporter dialed the phone number of the sheriff's newsline to listen to a recorded message (made by a sheriff's deputy) of law enforcement activities from the past twelve hours. After this, Slovekin made his routine morning check-in call to the city editor in the *Record* newsroom. Slovekin notified his boss of anything unusual happening on the beat, and the city editor told Slovekin of anything unusual happening in the newsroom. By now it would be about 7:50 AM. At some point during these twenty minutes at the sheriff's headquarters, the reporter would probably have picked up some additional news by chatting with any one of several people, including the watch officer on duty and the sheriff's information officer (whose job it was to supply the press with news).

After leaving the sheriff's department, the justice reporter arrived at the city police headquarters around 8:00 AM. He followed a similar routine here. First he went to his small cubicle with a writing surface, telephone, and typewriter. Next to the typewriter was the file of daily arrests and investigations of the city police. After looking through these (and taking notes or typing briefs), Slovekin walked into an adjoining room where he leafed through the daily traffic accident reports and read the police crime board (yet another place where police actions were listed). Finally, the reporter called the police newsline for a recorded message of more arrests and investigations.

By the time Slovekin left the police department and drove to the Purissima *Record*, it was 8:30 AM. The reporter immediately went to the city editor's desk, turned in his crime briefs, and conferred with his boss about what stories he would write and how much space he would have. He then went to his own desk to type up the daily "menu," a bureaucratic form (of use to the editors who put the paper together) specifying what stories that reporter would write for the day's edition of the newspaper, including an estimated length and a brief description of each story. After submitting the menu to the city editor, Slovekin headed off to the county courthouse to arrive by 9:00 AM when the superior courts opened.

The reporter first went to the court clerk's office to check the court calendar for the day. If he noticed any interesting case on the calendar, he would go to the specified courtroom to see if he could find out when the case would appear (the calendar did not have this information; he had to obtain it from a judge, bailiff, attorney, or simply by guessing). If he saw nothing particularly interesting in the calendar, he would go to the District 1 Courtroom of the presiding judge of superior court to watch the action. (According to the reporter, this courtroom was the most likely to have interesting cases because the presiding judge, who scheduled and assigned cases to other judges, would assign the "best" cases to himself.) During any lulls, the reporter might chat with attorneys, bailiffs, or law enforcement officers that he knew. He might also go to another courtroom to watch the proceedings or go back to the court clerk's office to check information in the case files. Generally, if the reporter was not observing a specific case that day, he spent his time in court snooping around for nothing in particular. By 10:00 or 10:30 AM Slovekin would return to the *Record* newsroom.

Back at his desk, Slovekin called the sheriff and the police newslines (after 10:00 AM these contained new material). He would also call back about any story he was going to write. Then he proceeded to type up stories from his notes. Meanwhile, Slovekin consulted with the city editor about any problems he was having writing a story or getting enough details on a story before the 12:30 PM deadline. Sometime just before noon the reporter called the watch officers at both the sheriff's and police departments to learn of any late-breaking news. Usually by 12:00 noon Slovekin would have all his stories written, and after handing them in he went to lunch. This was the end of his round, but not the end of his work day.

The first thing of note about the beat round is that it represents a routinized solution to the potentially recurring problem of how reporters gear their activities into two very differently organized domains of activities, those in the news organization and those in beat settings. All of the justice reporter's basic coverage work is accomplished well within the 12:30 PM writing deadline of his news organization. Simply by sticking to his round the reporter manages to "cover" Purissima's criminal justice system in a remarkably short period: one-half hour with the police, one-half hour with the sheriffs, and one hour at the courts. By 10:30 AM he has cycled through his round and is ready to fill his portion of news space. Later, in the discussion of what the reporter is actually monitoring in these agencies, we shall see how the round provides for such speedy coverage.

Even before 10:30 AM the reporter has been coordinating his activities with the needs of the editorial desk in the newsroom. Built into his round are two points at which the reporter communicates with the city editor. Both the 7:50 AM check-in call and the 9:00 AM news conference provide editor and reporter with the opportunity to reorient their work to the other's activities in the event that something is not routine on either end. If the city editor is faced with an unusually large or an unusually small amount of news space to fill, he will alert the reporter to write more or less than his routine amount of news copy. The city hall reporter described the significance of these constraints:

> It's like treating a pinball machine, you know. You shoot your story in [to the newsdesk] and the only thing that's going to get it out of there [to the composing room] is space and priority. If I write a story with a time element two days later, that's going to impact two days later, and there's a car wreck [on the freeway]—three people killed in it—then that'll bump my story, right? . . . The thing you keep in mind is that we all have a general idea when we start out in the morning how tight the paper is gonna be. We know how many news pages we've got. So if the city editor says, "Well, we have a very tight paper. Write it short," then you can hold it over, then you don't write stories that got three-day time elements. You just hold it. . . .
>
> I set up in my head my priority list and I will write only stories that will be in that paper . . . There's nothing set about this. [It's] my idea of what . . . has to get into the paper that day . . . Where I could write an eighteen-inch story I'll write a twelve-inch story. Where I could write a twelve-inch story I'll write an eight- or nine-inch story or a six-inch story. (Fishman interview 12-24-74, pp. 19, 23.)

On the other hand, if the beat reporter runs into "big news" on his round, he will need to alert his city editor that he will have to turn it in a half hour later than the 12:30 PM deadline. Whatever the circumstances, the round is organized in ways that allow both editor and reporter to orient their work to demands that the other faces.

The round shows the influences of the bureaucratically organized beat sources that the reporter follows. In particular, the sequence of stopping points on the round—from sheriffs to police to courts— takes on that order primarily because of the internal organization and scheduling of court activities relative to the organization of work in the two law enforcement agencies. Because the courts do not open until 9:00 AM, there is no reason to locate this stop on the beat any earlier. Moreover, court activities are organized such that no one, usually not even the judges, knows in advance precisely when a particular case will come before the bench. As a result, the reporter is left hanging around most of the time until something happens or it is time to leave for the newsroom. Because newsworkers loathe wasting their time, especially when god-knows-what is waiting for them on the rest of their beat, there is good reason to leave the courts as the last stopping place on the round.

In contrast to the courts, the reporter's news sources at the sheriffs' and police headquarters are highly dependable and freely available. These law enforcement agencies operate twenty-four hours a day: their files and personnel are available at any hour. The arrest, investigation, accident, and coroner's reports get updated at all hours, so it matters little at what point they are inspected. While the reporter can monitor these agencies at any time, the other fixed points on his beat—a 12:30 PM story deadline, an 11:00 AM starting time for assembling his materials, and the 9:00 AM court opening—push the two law enforcement agencies into the early morning hours of his round. The only apparent reason the reporter goes to the sheriff's station before the police department is their relative spatial locations. Because the police headquarters is located between the sheriff's department and the *Record*'s newsroom, the three points form a convenient driving route for that part of the round.

A second aspect of the round is that while my description of the justice reporter's round reads like a typical morning on the beat, it is more than that. It is also a description of his required morning of work. The round has a normative character. The routinization of the reporter's coverage in the form of a round is organizationally enforced. Reporters ignore this mode of coverage under the implicit penalty of job transfer, demotion, or firing and of damaging their reputations as competent journalists.

Moreover, to say that the round is normatively required is to say that what I have described as the justice beat round has the status of an "idealization" (Garfinkel 1967). That is, my description simplifies, typifies, idealizes what the reporter actually does on any given work day. Nevertheless, this picture of the round is part and parcel of the very beat work it typifies. The idealization is attached to the reporter's job. It is a description of what the reporter ought to do and what it looks like when it is done right. The reporter well knows the idealization of the round and so does the city editor and others who are familiar with the reporter on the beat. It is the reporter's own working knowledge of his or her movements through the beat territory. Reporters use the round-as-idealization to orient (or reorient) themselves and others to what they are doing on any particular occasion of cycling through the round. They employ the idealization to guide themselves through the very round which the idealization appears to describe. Reporters make the round happen because they are organizationally obliged to follow the sequence of typical actions that make up the idealization of their round.

But the idealization is more than a road map for the reporter's activities. It implicitly contains an ideology that continually informs the reporter what the beat is all about. As we shall see later, once reporters grasp the idealization of their round, other knowledge becomes part and parcel of their work. This includes such things as who on the beat is entitled to know what, who is an interested party, what occurrences fall outside the spectrum of potentially newsworthy events, what constitutes a controversy, and what constitutes all sides of a controversy.

The third major characteristic that should be noted about the round is that it does not provide for all the work activities of the reporter on the beat. The justice round occupies the justice reporter about half of his work day.[10] Even more significant, the round only specifies some of the places the reporter actually goes and some of the people and activities the reporter actually sees while engaged in the round. On any given day the justice reporter may meet particular sheriffs, policemen, judges, bailiffs, lawyers, and clerks who provide him with valuable information, and he may search certain files or attend special meetings that are not part of his daily work routine. In the course of cycling through the round, the reporter does a lot more than is specified in the idealization of the round. The idealized round simply provides the reporter with a minimum of places to go and people to see. In other words, the round maps out the basic coverage work of the beat. Upon this foundation more elaborate news contacts and more complex news gathering activities are built.

How does the round provide a foundation from which all the rest of the reporter's beat work proceeds? The round has a day-in-day-out repetitive character,[11] a stability over time. It consists of a series of locations that the reporter moves through in an orderly, scheduled sequence. When reporters first begin to follow a round on a regular basis, they establish themselves as fixtures within the territory of the beat. Over and over, their round leads them to the same locations at the same times. The reporter repeatedly sees the same people in the same places because these people's activities are organized such that they keep crossing paths with the reporter. People begin to recognize specific journalists, inquire who they are, and start up conversations with them. The possibility of forming relationships with these potential news sources is at hand. Moreover, where the reporter is going to be and when the reporter is there becomes common knowledge within the beat territory because the round makes the reporter's movements predictable, establishing the journalist as a locatable person. Any potential news source that wants to volunteer information knows where and when to find the reporter. Unsolicited tips and leads, from both total strangers and from familiar sources, turn out to be a significant resource in the journalist's investigative work.

The Bureaucratic Foundations of News Exposure

We can now return to the issue which brought us to examine the round in the first place. Just what are newsworkers systematically exposing themselves to by following a routine round of activities?

In the case of the justice reporter, the answer is clear: his information sources almost exclusively have a formally organized, governmental bureaucratic character. This generalization holds for the selectivity of the reporter's exposure at two different levels. First of all, at the broad-scale institutional level, the reporter regularly visited only bureaucratically organized settings. Out of the potentially infinite (and indefinite) expanse of his beat territory, Slovekin's round narrowed his coverage to three official agencies of social control: the city police, the county sheriffs, and the superior court. These three institutions represented only a portion of the formally constituted agencies functioning within the justice beat territory. The reporter's round simply excluded him from all juvenile facilities and adult penal institutions, the FBI branch office, two municipal police departments in the Purissima region, the local chapters of the American Civil Liberties Union, National Lawyer's Guild, and American Bar Association, a community legal collective, and all private security and detective agencies.[12] But more important than this, the justice round steered the reporter away from *all* institutions (or "communities of action") relevant to criminality and law enforcement which were not formally constituted or bureaucratically organized. Specifically, the journalist had no regular contact with the underlife of prisons and jails; the unofficially sanctioned practices of law enforcement, judicial, and penal personnel; the entire spectrum of deviant subcultures (from the world of winos to the stable corporate arrangements for price fixing); and the local markets for stolen goods, illegal drugs, and pornography.[13]

Second, focusing on the more concrete level of the journalist's specific sources of information, reporters expose themselves only to settings in which formally organized transactions of official business appear. That is, within the selected bureaucratic agencies that they do expose themselves to, again, the round selectively brings reporters before only bureaucratically organized presentations of activities. Within each agency, the justice reporter followed a very specific path that routed him to particular files, agency officials, and courtrooms. Notice how the reporter was covering each organization. By no means did he have them under surveillance nor was he "canvassing" the police, sheriffs, and courts. He did not move from office to office polling officials for news, nor did he observe "time slices" of their actual work. He did not ride in squad cars, and he would not hang around every courtroom in case something interesting transpired.

Rather, the justice reporter regularly exposed himself to only a few strategic points in each agency which were organizational foci of information within the criminal justice system. That is, the police, sheriffs, and courts all contained their own reporting systems, and the journalist routinely relied upon the products of these systems for doing his own work. The justice reporter routinely exposed himself to arrest and investigation reports, coroner's documents, traffic accident records, crime boards, newslines, court calendars, and court case files. Each of these were files recording the daily volumes of business received and processed by the police, sheriffs, and courts. From the reporter's point of view, he did not have to, nor would it necessarily have been possible to, witness the commission of crimes or the operations of law enforcement. The police, sheriffs, and courts recounted these events for him. Nor did the reporter need to ride in squad cars, observe autopsies, or be present at every court hearing. The police, sheriffs, and courts reported on what transpired in these places too. The reporter conveniently predicated his routine coverage on the fact that he could cash in on work already done for him by his beat agencies.

The informational foci of each agency are not only files, however. There are two other kinds of "centers" within agencies where diverse pieces of information are brought together or concentrated for the reporter. One of these information centers is in the form of a person: a member of the agency variously called the information officer, the community relations man, or the media contact. It is the job of such a person to approach the reporter routinely with potentially newsworthy information and to stand ready to consult with the reporter on information the journalist requires. On the justice beat, only the sheriff's department had such a full-time, officially designated position which the reporter regularly took advantage of. But even in agencies where an official press contact exists—and especially in agencies where one does not exist—the beat reporter relies upon other agency personnel who staff key outposts for the same purpose. Thus, the watch officer or the dispatcher in the sheriff's and police departments and the bailiffs in the courts were regular contacts within the justice reporter's round.

Another kind of informational focus included in the reporter's round is "the meeting." On each beat there are particular meeting places where formally organized, prescheduled activities take place which have the effect of concentrating diverse sources of information within a short period. In other words, when reporters routinely do expose themselves to ongoing activities (instead of exposing themselves to records of those activities), they invariably do so only in a place which guarantees that information formerly scattered throughout dozens of other settings will be brought together before them in that one setting. The city council meetings of the city hall reporter, the county board of supervisors' meeting of the county government reporter, and the District I Courtroom hearings of the justice reporter were all meetings which served this purpose and which were all obligatory stopping points on the reporters' rounds.

Whether their exposure consists of perusing particular files, talking with key agency personnel, or attending specific meetings, beat reporters cover an institutional locale by stationing themselves at those points at which masses of information collect. Governmental bureaucratic work is so organized that it makes observable to the reporter the topics of the beat, which were enacted in diverse parts of the beat territory, in a few centralized locations.

Usually it is not apparent when observing the reporter's daily routine that the round is the product of some active process for seeking out these concentrations of information. It simply looks like the journalist is following a well-worn path through each agency. While reporters themselves were generally unaware of how their beat rounds got created, there were a few episodes recorded in Wieder's field notes which reveal some of the work that goes into establishing a pattern which routes the reporter through new bureaucratic focal points of information. I would like to discuss one of these episodes in order to show what is involved in the establishment of new beat routines.

In the fall of 1964 the justice reporter was assigned the task of compiling a list of damages resulting from a large forest fire in the Purissima area. This was a major project which required several days' effort to locate and compile accounts of all the individual property damages. The reporter began by calling the public information office of the Forestry Service. This agency could only give the reporter a partial list of damages.

The city editor advised him [the police reporter] to call all the insurance offices where claims might possibly be filed. . . . [From the insurance companies the reporter was developing a new list of damages.] He checked his new list against the list he developed yesterday. This checking was important and was done at every stage of collecting these names and every time he got a list of names. Whether it was from the Forestry Service or elsewhere, they were checked for duplication. Now it appears that the reporter has high awareness that information is coming from various sets of activities, and that overlap between them is likely—also that duplication or repetition is counted as something quite bad in the newspaper. . . .

The reporter told me that . . . when he began [calling the insurance companies] he figured that there must be someplace where they would have all the information so that he wouldn't have to call all the individual insurance offices, and they told him about the General Adjustment Bureau [a central clearinghouse for all insurance claims in the area]. (Wieder field notes 10-2-64, p. 10.)

What is being described here is the reporter's continuing attempt to develop a network of sources relevant to the specific task at hand.[14] The work is particularly visible in this case because the reporter's task was one not accommodated by his already established network of sources in the justice beat round. He was forced to set up a new routine (a new segment on his round of activities) which would expose him to the phenomenon of interest (fire damages). While collecting the damage information the reporter was also engaged in a search for bigger and better sources: already existing records prepared and gathered by others for their own purposes. Specifically, when he discovered that the Forestry Service was not a sufficient source for property damage information, the reporter turned to other record-keeping agencies, namely, private insurance companies. This move in the search process was a move toward other bureaucracies and appears to have been guided by the following reasoning:

—What would any reasonable, rational individual with fire damages do such that all such individuals would do the same thing?

—And what would this thing be such that it would provide some central location for the information I am seeking?

The answer that satisfies both questions is that all reasonable parties would file damage claims with their insurance companies. To fill in this answer the reporter has to rely on his knowledge of standard social practices in his community. But, as the second question specifies, this knowledge of standard social practices must be of a particular sort. It is knowledge of how the social world is bureaucratically organized. The second half of the search procedure makes it clear that the journalist is looking for some agency which is already in a socially structured position to gather information about the phenomenon of interest.

Notice that the same twofold search procedure can be generalized to account for the reporter's next move toward establishing bigger and better information sources (i.e., finding the General Adjusting Bureau). After it became clear that telephoning every insurance office and double-checking each new list of damages against the other lists was going to be a slow and tedious process, the reporter seems to have applied the same reasoning process to locate an even more concentrated source of information: what would all reasonable insurance companies with fire damage claims do? And what would this be such that it would result in centralizing all their damage claims? They would report their claims to some sort of central clearinghouse because all reasonable insurance companies would have invented such a clearinghouse to coordinate (or guard against) paying off individuals who file multiple claims.

If we can assume that beat rounds get established in this manner (and, admittedly, the data are sparse on this subject), then we can see why those rounds invariably lead the reporter through bureaucratically organized concentrations of information. Of critical importance in explaining this is the general search procedure for establishing new information networks. The procedure continually invites reporters to treat all phenomena of interest as bureaucratically organized. It inevitably leads them to incorporate larger bureaucratic settings exclusively into their beat rounds. Novel tasks (such as compiling a list of fire damages) are routinized in a way that weds reporters to the largest bureaucratic reporting systems they can find. Thus, there is good reason to suspect that the historical development of reporters' routine beat rounds closely parallels the historical development of bureaucracy and its self-reporting apparatus.

All the essential characteristics of the round I have described for the justice beat apply in all beats observed on the Purissima *Record*. Significantly, the last feature I have been discussing—the exclusive bureaucratic character of what reporters regularly expose themselves to—is of general significance for any beat. Without exception, only formally constituted organizations and groups were the routine subjects of information gathering on beats. Whether these were neighborhood associations or federal agencies, the beat reporter was facing an already formed, systematically organized structure of activities and information.

It comes as no great surprise that the city hall and county government beats dealt on a regular basis almost entirely with the bureaucracies of city and county administrative departments, regulatory bodies, and legislative councils, boards, commissions, and committees. When reporters were not monitoring the files and attending the meetings of these officials, they were attending the scheduled, agenda-bound meetings of formally constituted citizens' groups. As the county beat reporter summed up the pattern of exposure to the newsworld, "This beat as it was set up when I came into it—and I haven't changed it that much—is very meeting-oriented." (Fishman field notes 7-21-74, p. 3.) This may even be an understatement. The county beat round consisted of regularly attending the meetings of some fourteen different governmental bodies. On average, this reporter spent three and three-quarters days out of a five-day work week watching meetings. (That is 75 percent of the work week and over six meetings per week.) And this does not count the reporter's time—still part of the round—for checking specific files, dropping in on particular officials in their offices, and composing news stories. Virtually all of the county reporter's exposure to the beat was fixed through the round—a round which overwhelmingly displayed the world of local government through official meetings. The county reporter was aware that this way of covering the beat meant seeing mostly bureaucratically packaged events:

Most of my time is spent in meetings . . . . There are days that have no meetings—maybe one or two days a week. And when I don't have a meeting it frees me to talk to people about things that are going on. *A lot of times there are things going on, and by the time they get to a meeting they're pretty well wrapped up.* (Fishman field notes 7-21-74, p. 4; emphasis added.)

Whatever went on backstage that led up to the packaging of actual governmental work in the form of an agenda item was lost to the county beat reporter who was chained to meetings through the round.[15] And the reporter knew it. Moreover, interviews with other beat reporters show they shared the same sentiments that a good deal is lost by sitting in meetings watching a parade of staged presentations. According to the city hall reporter,

The city council meeting Tuesday—that's to me a full day lost. You know, I would consider that a day lost because . . . you have to sit there for so long and listen to so much meaningless conversation." (Fishman interview 12-24-73, p. 3.)

Beat reporters eventually develop enough familiarity with the backstage of meetings to know that the organization and staging of business in terms of agenda items is intended to reconstruct the actual work of agency decision making: to reformulate it along the lines of standard procedure, to clean it up, to summarize it, and to disguise it. It is with reference to this known discrepancy between actual work and staged appearances that reporters are able to sense the meaninglessness of the presentations.

But the justice, city hall, and county beat reporters were not exceptional in their systematic exposure to bureaucratic settings. It simply made no difference what the topic of beat coverage was. For instance, the environment beat occupied its reporter in meetings as much as the city hall and county government beats did. Even the *Record*'s nature beat, which produced stories about the local mountain area, forests, and wildlife, depended on the Forestry Service for its news. When it turned out that even rocks, trees, and squirrels are made available to the newspaper through official agencies, then it is no exaggeration to say that *the world is bureaucratically organized for journalists.*

The journalist's view of the society as bureaucratically structured is the very basis upon which the journalist is able to detect events. Such a perspective on the newsworld provides the reporter with a means for locating knowledge of particular happenings in the society that have already occurred. Upon hearing of a large warehouse fire, one knows that the local fire department is in a position to have the information. Upon being notified of a double suicide, one knows that the police are in a position to know the details. Whatever the happening, there are officials and authorities in a structural position to know.

But more importantly, this perspective of a bureaucratically structured society provides the journalist, in advance of any particular occurrence, with a map of relevant knowers for any topic of newsworthy happenings. Suppose the topic is criminality and law enforcement. Who would be in a position to know such happenings once they occurred? The police and the courts. Suppose the topic is nuclear attack. Who then would be in a position to know? The city and county civil defense agencies. Once newsworkers see the community as bureaucratically structured, they have at their disposal a powerful perspective which informs them of who is in a position to know virtually anything they want to know. This bureaucratic consciousness is invaluable for detecting news because it indicates where the reporters should position themselves to discover happenings not yet known.

Moreover, these structural locations provide for the continuous detection of events. This is quite important to the newsworker. Remember that reporters are under a relentless obligation to produce dependable quantities of news daily, no matter how much or how little they feel is happening. In practical terms this means that beat reporters need stable sources which generate reliable quantities of information. This is precisely what a bureaucratic self-reporting apparatus assures. Through thick and thin, day after day, journalists know where and when they can get information, and they know there will be fresh material there.

It is quite understandable, then, why the beat round so heavily focuses on bureaucratic "fountains of information."[16] The reporter can expect these fountains to flow reliably because their operation is normatively enforced within the agencies the reporter observes. It is as much a part of the bureaucrat's job to report on things that they do as it is to do those things in the first place. Thus, the same way in which the readers of a newspaper can depend on predictable quantities of news reports day after day, reporters can depend on the bureaucratic reporting apparatus for their raw materials. The dependability of the operations of both reporting systems, bureaucratic and journalistic, is normatively enforced within the organizations that encompass them.

The structure of the reporter's news gathering work (the round) is shaped by the bureaucratic organization of the activities within the beat territory. The substance of what reporters gather (bureaucratically packaged activities) is produced within the agencies they cover. Whatever the sphere of human activity or natural occurrences, as long as it is systematically covered through the beat, the newsworker sees it from a round and knows it through officials and authorities, their files, and their meetings. Quite literally the domain of coverage is produced for the newsworker in formally organized settings by clerks, forest rangers, policemen, stock brokers, councilmen, morticians, and judges—all certified status incumbents in structural positions of knowledge. In and by their work these organizational actors establish structures of knowledge consisting of what there is to know in the first place (possible knowledge) and who knows what, where, and when (distributed knowledge). These local structures of knowledge are what reporters must understand, take into account, and manipulate, not only to guide themselves through their beat, but also to interpret what they are exposed to. Let us now turn to this latter use of bureaucratic knowledge structures as schemes of interpretation.

3. Seeing News Events

The Interpretation of Activities

It is one thing for a reporter to be in a position of exposure to activities on the beat. Following the round insures this. It is quite another thing for reporters to know what to make of the activities to which they are exposed. At 7:30 in the morning the justice round provides the police reporter with stacks of arrest and investigation reports. In what way is one supposed to see "events" in these pieces of paper? At 9:00 AM every Tuesday the city hall reporter, in accordance with his round, is watching another city council meeting go by. Where are the events in the endless talk, gestures, and reports? In short, what sort of scheme of interpretation is the reporter employing on the beat in order to understand what is going on and to discern events out of complicated displays of activities? Because an event is an interpreted phenomenon, something organized in thought, talk, and action, it can only be an event *for somebody*. On what basis do newsworkers routinely see events? My ethnographic evidence shows that journalists perceive events in substantially the same way that beat agency officials formulate their own and other persons' activities as events.

Within formal organizations (regardless of whether reporters cover them on a beat), complexes of activities are organized into events on the basis of a few specific schemes of interpretation—what I shall call phase structures. When beginning work in a new beat, the novice reporter is confronted with an established domain of typical events. For example, on the justice beat typical events were arrests, sentencings, preliminary hearings, plea bargains, and arraignments. These were not encountered as a loose collection of event categories but were seen as interrelated in a highly structured scheme. Typical events were organized along a sort of timeline or career path. The police reporter saw crime news events as organized around legal cases, each of which progressed through a fixed sequence of phases: first the arrest, then the preliminary hearing, then arraignment, and so on until the final phase of sentencing. Each phase defined a possible news event. The entire sequence of phases was a phase structure portraying streams of interwoven activities as an object moving through a series of stages, or as a case moving through a career. Before I elaborate on this let us examine the concept of phase structures more closely.

Common Sense Phase Structures

The use of phase structures for interpreting events is not peculiar to journalists or to the agency personnel on the reporter's beat. It is a very general scheme employed in everyday thought for picturing events in the context of successively developing phases. How might any of us carve up happenings into a phase structure? Take the case of a missing child. In telling the story about what happened, it is common to organize an account in terms of some chain of events: "Around noon Mrs. Smith couldn't find her little girl Lulu anywhere. Finally, after four hours of searching, Lulu was found two blocks away hiding in a neighbor's yard." Such an account can be depicted as the series of events in Figure 1A. This is an example of a phase structure because it organizes an amorphous something into a determinate sequence of events. However, this structuring could be done in other ways. For example, the story could be more elaborate: "When Mrs. Smith came home at noon she couldn't find Lulu. She looked all over the house and the neighborhood and after two hours phoned the police. The police then searched the neighborhood until 4:00, when they found Lulu hiding in a neighbor's yard two blocks away from Mrs. Smith's house." As this version is depicted in Figure 1B, there are more phases: an antecedent phase (parent comes home) is tacked on to the beginning of the story, and the single search phase of Figure 1A is now specified as two phases in Figure 1B (parent searches and police search).

Yet a third version could be given in which even earlier and later events are recounted, while other events are left out: "The night before his daughter ran away, Mr. Smith spanked Lulu for stealing candy from a drug store. At noon the next day Lulu was nowhere to be found. Mrs. Smith looked all over the neighborhood and after two hours phoned the police. The police then looked all over the neighborhood until 4:00 when they found Lulu hiding in a neighbor's yard two blocks away from Mrs. Smith's house. That night Mr. Smith spanked Lulu again for running away from home." Figure

Figure 1. Three common sense phase structures

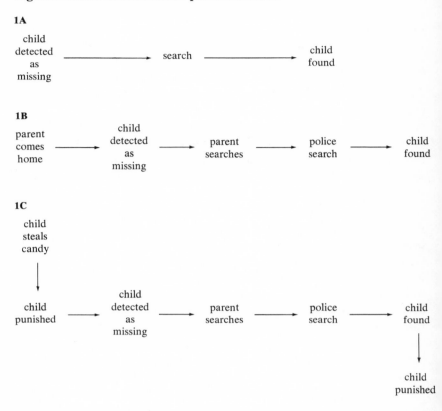

1c depicts this story, showing the exclusion of the parent-comes-home stage, but the inclusion of two even earlier stages (child steals candy and child punished) and one even later stage (child punished).

These various ways in which members of society, using everyday reasoning, can carve up reality illustrate several basic properties of common sense phase structures.

1. The specific phases delimiting the structure are somewhat arbitrary. The structure could be outlined in a variety of plausible ways. More or less detail in the event career could be emphasized by adding or subtracting phases. Moreover, it is always plausible to

extend the structure at either end by adding earlier beginning phases and later ending phases.

2. Each phase in the structure designates an event. Phase structures mark action units (events) out of a stream of ongoing activities. Taking this point together with the first point, we can see that the complex of activities associated with a missing child can be formulated as a variety of events: from the single event "child missing" to an indefinite number of successive events.

3. Phases occur in sequential order. Phases occurring out of order spoil the entire phase structure, calling into question all phases as not what they appear to be, as not genuine events. If a child is found before he or she is noticed as missing, the child really could not have been missing at all, nor, for that matter, could the child really have been found. Thus, the sequential property of the entire phase structure is defined by its component events. An event is not an event if it appears out of order. This sequential characteristic has its advantages: once one knows the present phase of a case, one can tell what events happened before and what events are likely to happen next in its career.

4. Phases have typical durations in time. There are expectable and reasonable amounts of time between entry into a present phase and entry into the next phase. Thus, it is not unreasonable for hours to transpire between the time a child runs away from home and the time the child is noticed as missing. But if this duration were in months or years, then something would be drastically wrong. Similarly, if the search phase were to last only a few seconds, the entire phase structure would be invalidated. Inappropriate phase durations can signal: (1) that there is really no event after all (How can a child really be "missing" for twelve seconds?), or (2) that the happenings are a different kind of thing than they originally appeared to be because the actors in the events have a bad moral character (What kind of parents would take two years to realize that their child was missing? This must be a case of an abandoned child not a missing child.).

5. There is a continuity between phases. Each phase develops out of its preceding phase along a continuum. There is a certain sameness to events throughout the entire phase structure. As the object

moves through the sequence of phases, it is in agreement with itself at each phase and throughout all phases of its career. The missing child is the selfsame person and the selfsame case at the run-away-from-home stage as at the found stage. It would defy common sense if the runaway child turned up three days later at the found stage as a forty-seven-year-old bearded dockworker. The fundamental implausibility here arises because, in common sense terms, no continuous stream of developing activities could be supplied which would fill in the three day gap such that the object at the first phase (missing child) is in agreement with the object at the second phase (forty-seven-year-old bearded dockworker). One important consequence of the presumed continuity within phase structures is that this feature invites users of the scheme to fill in the likely or typical events which connect two separate phases in the structure. Thus, it is common sense to assume that a missing child who was found three days after disappearing also was searched for in the interim.

Bureaucratic Phase Structures and News Phase Structures

Although journalists employ common sense phase structures, I found that beat reporters rely heavily upon a few special phase structures, which I term bureaucratic phase structures because they originate from and are in common use within the specific agencies on reporters' rounds. Bureaucratic phase structures describe events as they are formally produced and processed by the bureaucracies the reporter covers. They also represent the reporter's own basic knowledge of typical events on the beat.

Reporters come to know the particular bureaucratic phase structures of their beats intimately. I found that all beat reporters could recite them from memory. Here is how the justice reporter described the central phase structure of his police court beat:

It's very simple. I suppose you know it starts with the arrest. I think that's basic. You should have an arrest to run a crime story. And then, in theory, it would end . . . with the sentencing . . . . That's really for our purposes where it would end. So I would see it when a person's arrested and see it on the police report. And then I would know there was a number of different court stops along the way. There'd be the [municipal court] preliminary hearing . . . at which the question arises, would the person be held up for superior court . . . . And of course you have more than one of these if the case is complicated. Normally it's just a few minutes in the morning, and away he goes to superior court, since very few [felonies] are dismissed in municipal court. If it goes to superior court, you know, two days or two weeks later you know that he will appear in which he will be arraigned. He will plead, you know, "I plead not guilty." And then you always know there'll be a readiness and settlement hearing at which they [the prosecuting and defending attorneys] talk about a plea bargain. And when that is reached, if they agree on a plea bargain,[1] which is frequent, three weeks then elapse so the probation department has time to prepare a report for the guidance of the judge who sentences him. But the normal thing is that there are continuances, there are delays, requests by the D. A., requests by the defense, for these continuances. So it can, may take actually several months. (Fishman interview 3-19-74, p. 5.)

Figure 2 simplifies the police reporter's verbal description in a diagram. Let us use this particular case to illustrate the features of bureaucratic and news phase structures.

Figure 2. Justice reporter's news phase structure

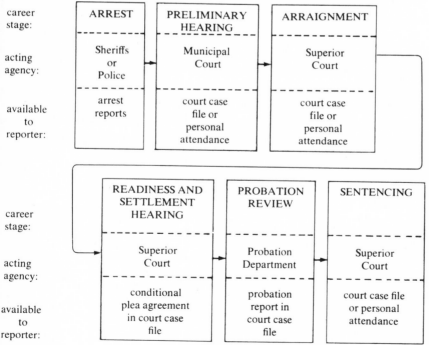

First, note the encompassing nature of the police court phase structure. It connects the activities of all three beat agencies on the reporter's round: the police, sheriffs, and courts. What is most interesting about a phase structure like this is that phases are officially precategorized—each with a formal title—and are finite in number. Common sense phase structures have a variable number of phases (each with an indefinite number of plausible titles); by contrast, bureaucratic phase structures formulate events and formalize their number, names, and sequence. The primary news events in Purissima's world of criminality and law enforcement are arrests, preliminary hearings, arraignments, plea bargains, probation reviews, and sentencings.

Although this way of formulating and dividing up a stream of activities as events is clearly taken from a bureaucratic perspective, the justice reporter's version of the police court phase structure does not completely correspond with the police, sheriff's, and court's versions of the phase structure. For example, the police and sheriffs, in doing their work, would have to picture the beginning of the phase structure starting at an earlier phase and containing more phases, something like Figure 3.

In general, news phase structures tend to be truncated, less detailed versions of bureaucratic phase structures. The justice reporter alludes to this in his verbal description of the police court phase structure. When he says, "It starts with the arrest. You should have an arrest to run a crime story. . . . In theory it would end with the sentencing. That's really for our purposes where it would end," he is telling us this is an event scheme for the reporter's purposes.

Figure 3A. Police and sheriff's bureaucratic phase structure

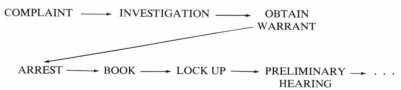

```
COMPLAINT ———→ INVESTIGATION ———→ OBTAIN
                                  ╱ WARRANT
                               ╱
                            ╱
ARREST ———→ BOOK ———→ LOCK UP ———→ PRELIMINARY —→ . . .
                                    HEARING
```

Figure 3B. Reporter's news phase structure

```
ARREST ——————————→ PRELIMINARY —→ . . .
                    HEARING
```

News phase structures tend to be derived from bureaucratic phase structures. And bureaucratic phase structures are similar to common sense phase structures. Bureaucratic schemes display the same basic properties of common sense schemes but with two important exceptions. First of all, the specific phases delimiting the bureaucratic phase structure are not arbitrary but are bureaucratically provided and bureaucratically enforced. Events are formally fixed and specified in the normal and proper operating procedures of the agency. Second, the three properties of common sense phase structures—continuity between phases, sequential organization of phases, and typical durations of phases—are all present in bureaucratic phase structures. But unlike common sense phase structures, these properties are, again, bureaucratically produced by agency personnel; that is, the sameness of the case throughout its various phases is created in the way that it is defined and processed by agency personnel throughout its various phases. Similarly, the specific sequential order of phases and their typical durations are made to happen by bureaucrats' following proper procedures.

Despite the differences between news phase structures and bureaucratic phase structures, news phase structures are still derivatives of bureaucratic phase structures. Bureaucratic schemes are but one perspective on the chain of events associated with any actual case. For example, an individual taken into the criminal justice system as a suspect would most certainly organize his or her own experiences differently from the way an agency official or a journalist would. Event phases for the suspect could include such matters as betrayal to the police by a friend-turned-informer, the whole gamut of experiences in jail, formulation of a legal defense with an attorney, and so on. These kinds of personal or nonbureaucratic phase structures have received considerable attention in the sociological literature on "careers," both deviant and nondeviant. Most notably, Goffman's studies of moral careers (1961, 1963) and Roth's work on timetables (1963) show the way in which clients, patients, and prisoners organize sets of experiences under institutional and noninstitutional conditions.

Although alternative formulations of activities may abound in the places reporters cover, the journalist's sense of events comes not from clients' oral histories (as it did for Goffman and Roth) but from official case histories. Journalists simply do not expose themselves regularly to unofficial interpretive schemes. For example, the justice reporter steered clear of suspects, victims, and their families on his round. The only routine occasion in which the reporter was exposed to the suspect's version of events was during formal court hearings. But these were settings in which the suspect's version necessarily had been reformulated through an attorney to fit the legal-bureaucratic definition of events. In general, reporters in courtrooms will seek out lawyers, not their clients, as news sources.

Why do newsworkers so readily adopt a bureaucratic definition of events? Why are news phase structures patterned after bureaucratic phase structures? We already have a partial answer: through their rounds beat reporters systematically and exclusively expose themselves to formally organized settings which present them with bureaucratically packaged activities. More can be said about this now.

Notice that the object or case moving through a bureaucratic phase structure is made to move through its career by agency personnel. Arrests do not just happen. They are accomplished by the activities of patrolmen, detectives, dispatchers, secretaries, and the like. Similarly, arraignments are produced through the work of lawyers, judges, bailiffs, clerks, and so forth. The career path is accomplished in the bureaucratic processing of the case; the object being dealt with becomes a formal entity, a legal-bureaucratic case. Its treatment within each phase and its movement into each new phase are specified by agency procedures and accomplished by the decisions and actions of agency personnel. And it is their job to do this, to make the object look like a case and to make its processing look like the movement of a case through a bureaucratic phase structure. To do this, agency personnel must use the phase structure as a guide for dealing with the case: What phase is it in now? What are the standard procedures for it in this phase? Where does it go next?

In short, for agency personnel a bureaucratic phase structure is a normatively required idealization of a chain of events which, in turn, is employed by those personnel to produce the very chain of events pictured in the idealization. As idealizations, bureaucratic phase structures are productive of the same sequence of events they describe. Just as the reporter's routine is idealized as a round, so is the work in agencies within the beat idealized as phases in a phase structure.

Reporters employ phase structures as schemes for interpreting bureaucratic activities, just as the bureaucrats they observe employ them to produce the activities reporters see. In other words, phase structures are schemes for action as well as schemes for interpretation—schemes for doing and schemes for seeing. If the reporter does not learn the specific phase structures of the beat, she or he cannot understand at the simplest level what is happening there. If the reporter has not grasped the same scheme that beat officials use in doing their everyday work, then he or she has no way of telling what they are up to as they see it, what they mean by what they are doing. Failure to understand this would amount to serious journalistic incompetence. After a few stories that betrayed such ignorance, the reporter would be transferred off the beat. For the journalist, bureaucratic phase structures are socially sanctioned schemes of interpretation.

The Uses of Phase Structures

News phase structures are of much wider use to journalists than the mere passive understanding of what's going on within the beat territory. My field observations show a variety of uses to which reporters put bureaucratically defined news phase structures. Let us examine what happened when the justice reporter encountered a fairly typical newsworthy case on his round. The incident in my field observations began in the county courthouse where the reporter was covering superior court cases.

9:10 AM

We go to Department 1, the courtroom of the presiding judge of superior court, Judge Bennett. A case has already begun. There is a black woman standing before the judge. She is flanked by her lawyer (the public defender) and the assistant district attorney. She has apparently pleaded guilty to something because the judge is carefully explaining to her exactly what her guilty plea means, i.e., her rights. The judge periodically asks her if she understands. Then he asks the assistant D. A. if the terms of her guilty plea are acceptable to him. He says yes. The terms are that she changes her plea of not guilty for assaulting a police officer to a plea of guilty for interfering with a police officer. Thirty seconds into this whole process the justice reporter Slovekin suddenly recognizes the case: "Oh, I know what this is. It's really interesting." He is excited, and listens intently, occasionally taking notes. He says he will tell me about it later. . . .

[After observing another case] Slovekin and I leave the courtroom to go to talk in a small room in the courthouse. . . . Slovekin explained to me about the case where the woman pleaded guilty to the lesser charge. He said her name was Martha Mungan, and that she was a major character in a big crime story a few months ago, and that her case had finally reached the courts. Slovekin added that it was only by chance that he had happened on it today: it did not show up on the court calendar which he had looked at earlier. The story of Martha Mungan according to Slovekin is this:

Last December late one night Martha Mungan was drinking with her common-law husband, and they got into a fight. Very drunk, she got out her husband's two guns and went outside. She was threatening people with the weapons until someone called the police. The police were alerted to go to her husband's address where there was an armed woman. When the cops arrived, she was standing across the street pointing two guns at them. The police pulled their guns, pointing them at her, shouting for her to drop her weapons. It was a tense situation until her husband came out of the house yelling at her to drop the guns. Instead, she raised them at the police. The officers opened fire, wounding her. Her husband grabbed the guns, fired at the police, wounding one cop; the police shot back, killing the husband. Martha Mungan was arrested. They determined she was heavily drunk while her husband was only slightly intoxicated. There was an inquest at which the police were exonerated of any wrongdoing.

Now Martha Mungan's case had finally come up, and Slovekin said he was very interested in what would happen to her since she had been the cause of the whole thing. He said that what we had just seen was the readiness and settlement hearing. He noted that the original charge of assaulting a policeman was very serious, and its reduction to interfering with a policeman was substantial. He heard the judge say that this lesser charge has a prescribed five-year sentence, which Slovekin considers a major sentence. But he added that it all depends on how the judge sentences her when the hearing comes up. Slovekin is interested in seeing what sentence she actually gets because "it's unusual for a woman to go to prison."

10:30 AM

We walk back to the newsroom and Slovekin goes immediately to the city editor's desk. The city editor tells him that Peter Colton, the county D. A. (and political enemy of the Purissima *Record*) personally called up the newspaper to tell the city editor and Slovekin [who was on his round at the time] that the Martha Mungan case was going to be in court and what the plea bargain would be. As Colton went into the details, the city editor told him to hold off until he talked to Slovekin. Both the city editor and Slovekin noted to each other how remarkable it was that the D. A. had called the paper to be so helpful, speculating that Colton might be trying to ingratiate himself with the newspaper just before his up-coming reelection campaign. Then Slovekin told the city editor how he happened to catch the case in court, even though it was not on the calendar, and that he had all the details already. The city editor told Slovekin he wanted the Martha Mungan guilty plea story for the home edition deadline (12:30 PM). Slovekin said he had thought he would not write anything now but wait for the sentencing of Martha Mungan (due in a few weeks). The city editor did not respond. Slovekin went back to his desk to write up the story. The story he wrote appeared on the second page of the local news section of the day's home edition as follows:

WOMAN PLEADS IN SHOOTOUT CASE

Martha Mungan pleaded guilty today to a charge stemming from a predawn shootout last December that left her wounded and her common-law husband dead from police bullets.

Mrs. Mungan pleaded guilty to one count of threatening and interfering with police officers, and a second count was dismissed.

Her sentencing was set for March 22 in the court of Superior Judge Lloyd Bennett.

Police were called to Mrs. Mungan's home at 410-B Oceano Ave. last December by Rodney Charles Harvey, her common-law husband, during a family fight. In the ensuing gunfight, Mrs. Mungan was wounded and Harvey was killed when he retrieved the pistols and shot at police.

10:40 AM

[While Slovekin is writing this story] I go downstairs where the city editor is on a break. I asked him why he wanted the Martha Mungan story now instead of when Slovekin wanted it. He said, "Just my own judgment. Because it's news." He added that the question of whether to do the story now or at the sentencing time was not a big deal but that he wanted something now because the background of the case was interesting and the fact that it was a negotiated plea made it newsworthy as well: "Plea bargaining is a hot issue now." I asked him if another story would be done for the sentencing. He said, "Definitely." He added that by doing a story now at the plea bargaining stage the next story at the sentencing stage would be a followup. As he put it, "People want to know what happens to this thing." (Fishman field notes 2-28-74, pp. 6–9.)

At the beginning of this incident we see that the reporter actually encountered the newsworthy event of Martha Mungan's guilty plea in a sort of "aha experience." There was a sudden recognition of what the court activities meant by seeing them as constituting one phase in the larger career of the Martha Mungan case. In other words, the reporter saw the activities as a newsworthy event as soon as he saw the bureaucratic phase structure to which they belonged.

But he did more than simply recognize the event by means of a phase structure scheme. The reporter treated the entry of the case into a new phase (the readiness and settlement hearing) as a possible occasion for writing a news story. Both Slovekin and his city editor assumed as a matter of course not only that the readiness and settlement hearing called for a news story, but also that the next expected phase in the case's career, the sentencing, provided the next occasion for a news story. Clearly, news stories are occasioned by the recognized movement of a case into a new phase in its event career. I found this to be true for all beat reporters throughout the period of study.

Phase structures provide reporters with the sense that something new is happening. This solves an important problem for journalists. One important component of the newsworthiness of any story is that a story must be timely. News is considered a highly perishable commodity (Park 1940: 676; Tuchman 1973: 118; Roshco 1975: 10–11). It must be published recently with respect to the occurrence of an event. But what is meant by the occurrence of an event? After all, most objects of news coverage are occurring all the time. Martha Mungan is an active case whether she is standing before a judge, sitting in jail, or conferring with her lawyer. Antitrust suits develop over a period of several years through a succession of investigations and court hearings. Legislative issues can continue over months and years of public debate, backroom agreements, and official voting. Even so-called spot news events like floods, plane crashes, oil spills, and nerve gas leaks can take months before a full account of what took place surfaces. How does the journalist know at what points the continuing activities warrant a story? When do the activities become timely enough to be written about? Bureaucratic phase structures solve this problem because they provide the resource for reporters to sense when something new is happening. A continuing story occurs whenever the issue enters a new phase, i.e., when it crosses a boundary between phases.

This does not mean that every time a case moves across a phase structure boundary it will get written up as a news story. Rather, the movement of a case warrants a news story. It justifies for reporters and their superiors the reporting of the story at that time. In the journalist's own terms, the occasion which warrants the writing of a story is called a "news peg" or "news hook" (Crouse 1974: 115, 240). My findings indicate that news pegs coincide with bureaucratically defined phase structure boundaries. Reporters' bureaucratically organized universe not only defines their movements through the beat territory, their exposure to news sources, and the form and content of news events. It also defines the permissible times at which an event may be reported. Newsworkers' very concept of the timeliness of news is based in the phase structure schemes the agencies on their beats provide.

Journalists plan the reporting of future news events around bureaucratically defined news pegs. We saw in the Martha Mungan incident that individually, and in interaction with each other, both Slovekin and the city editor expressed interest in doing a story when the case reached the sentencing stage. Moreover, both Slovekin and the city editor kept their own date books (sometimes called future files) in which they kept track of future newsworthy events. Thus, each noted Martha Mungan's expected sentencing in their date books just before the page for March 22 (when the judge said she would appear again). All reporters keep such files on cases or issues which they expect to appear more than once. The city editor also would keep a future file to remind himself (and one of his reporters, if he felt it was necessary) of what should be covered on any given day.

Notice that with the publication of successive stories about a case, the newsworker establishes a sense of continuing news. Tuchman (1973: 115) found, and my observations confirm, that the journalist's concept of continuing news is "a series of stories *on the same subject* based upon events occurring over a period of time." The very concept of continuing news is grounded in bureaucratically organized schemes in which cases move through phase structures. Reporters treat each individual story as the next installment of one big continuing story. In fact, each next installment is conveniently scheduled for them by the agencies on their beats. Because bureaucracies establish their own timetables for processing cases and because newsworkers identify news phase structures with bureaucratic phase structures, reporters are able to know in advance when, where, and roughly what will happen with an event which has yet to occur.

> Continuing news *facilitates* the control of work, for continuing news events are generally prescheduled. Prescheduling is implicit in the newsman's definition of continuing news as a "series of stories on the same subject based upon events occurring over a period of time." This definition implies the existence of prescheduled change. . . .
>
> Because they are prescheduled, continuing news stories help newsmen and news organizations to regulate their own activities; they free newsmen to deal with the exigencies of the specifically unforeseen (Tuchman 1973: 123).

Tuchman (1973: 123) poses a relevant question here for future research: "How do newsmen decide that two events are about the 'same topic'?" Once we see that the concept of continuing news is based upon the phase structure scheme of interpretation, then it is clear that the sameness of the story's topic is provided for in one of the basic properties of all phase structures discussed earlier. Namely, there must be continuity between phases, and this means that the object moving through its phases must be in agreement with itself (i.e., be the same case) throughout different phases. Because journalists tend to rely on bureaucratically defined phase structures, the case (the story's topic or subject) is identical with itself throughout all phases because bureaucrats make it appear as the same case and treat it as the same case at all phases.

Tuchman convincingly demonstrates that newsworkers endeavor to routinize the unexpected. My research shows how a key portion of the newsworld (beat agencies) provides the resource for that routinization.

Just how journalists actively produce a sense of continuing news in their use of bureaucratic phase structures is important to note. Recall that when I asked the city editor why he had decided to publish stories for both phases in the Martha Mungan case (the plea bargain and sentencing), he indicated that by running stories at both phases the second story would be a followup of the first. Deciding to do a story now in order that it can be followed up later is not only a way for newsworkers to create (for readers and for themselves) a sense that there is a continuing story; it is also a method for displaying complete or thorough coverage of the continuing story. The way in which the city editor made his decision is an unexpected finding in light of how most students of the media (as well as newspaper readers) assume followup decisions happen. Typically, it is assumed that the decision to follow up is made only after some original event has been covered. However, it works in a very different way (almost the other way around). The decision to do a followup story was made as part of the same decision to do the original story. One of the city editor's considerations for doing the original story (on the plea bargain) was that it would display the future story (on the sentencing) as followup news. Because there was never any question between Slovekin and the city editor that the future sentencing story would be done, it is almost as if the decision to do the followup story was made before the decision to do the original story.

Over and above the use of bureaucratic phase structures to occasion news stories, reporters employ these interpretive schemes in another important way. Once journalists have adopted a bureaucratic frame of reference, they possess a convenient means for spotting the highlights of events. One of the striking features of bureaucratic phase structures is their consistent orientation toward the disposition of the case. Each event or phase is procedurally organized around some decision to be made or action to be taken which settles the case for the time being (and that usually means sending it on to its next phase, if there is one). This disposition of the case is seen as the key or central activity within each phase. The reason for this is not hard to understand. Insofar as journalists (or bureaucrats) see something as a case moving through a phase structure, then their interest is bound to focus on the disposition of the case, as bureaucratic cases only exist so that they can be properly disposed of. In short, the orientation of phase structures toward the bureaucratic disposition of the case provides the newsworker with a ready-made scheme of relevance.[2]

The justice reporter's coverage of the Martha Mungan case nicely illustrates this. After encountering the case in court, Slovekin told me he was very interested in what would happen to her. His primary interest was couched in terms of the ultimate disposition of her case in the court system (i.e., when the case moved out of the territory of his beat): What would the judge's sentence be? Slovekin's immediate practical interest was couched in terms of her most recent disposition at the plea bargaining stage: What were the results of the bargaining? This is particularly clear in the way Slovekin wrote up the event. His lead sentence, in classic journalistic style, stated (along with some background information) the most important aspect of the event, namely, its disposition. Martha Mungan pleaded guilty, and this guilty plea defined the disposition of the case as a result of the readiness and settlement hearing. Similarly, Slovekin's second paragraph elaborated on this disposition by stating what she pleaded guilty to.

But notice that nowhere in the story was there any mention of the fact that Martha Mungan's plea was a negotiated plea.[3] Only someone who was both an experienced reader of the newspaper and an experienced observer of the court system would deduce a negotiated plea from the facts that she pleaded guilty, that a charge was dismissed, and that all this happened at this stage of her judicial career. Rarely do journalists report negotiated pleas as negotiated pleas, even though they will write feature stories, news analyses, and editorials about negotiated pleas in the abstract. It is mainly the guilty plea itself which is newsworthy because it represents a disposition of the case. That the plea was bargained over is a detail which, more often than not, is omitted in brief news reports focusing on how defendants plead.[4]

I found this same phenomenon of focusing on the dispositions of cases on the other beats as well. On the city hall and county government beats the key actions within city council and board of supervisors meetings were the formal legislative dispositions of issues, which usually meant the results of voting. Pleading guilty to interfering with a police officer, getting sentenced to two years in prison, voting down a raise in the property tax, and passing a new loitering ordinance are all bureaucratically appropriate dispositions as well as the stuff of which routine news stories are made.

Because the most relevant feature of the event is the disposition of the case, all other features of the event are of secondary importance. They become the details which are defined by and revolve around the central fact of the case's actual disposition. The bargaining process that produced the guilty plea, the judge's lecture to the sentenced prisoner, the defendant's reasons for interfering with the police, the arguments for and against the legislative issue, the behind-the-scenes lobbying which arranged the voting—these are all details which embellish the basic event. By focusing on bureaucratically appropriate dispositions in their everyday reports, journalists' stories leave invisible the agency procedures and social conditions which give rise to these dispositions. Routine news stories implicitly support the status quo by taking for granted these background factors. The report of Martha Mungan's guilty plea rendered the procedure of plea bargaining unproblematic by obscuring it. Even less visible were the social conditions of Martha Mungan's life (as a ghetto resident) which surrounded the incident which made her into a judicial case in the first place.

The point is not that such background factors are never reported. Rather, they are rarely given attention in routine stories precisely because they are considered background vis à vis a foreground of the bureaucratic disposition of the case. And when these factors become prominent in a story, they are not reported as routine news. Such stories are relegated to the status of feature news, human interest stories, news analysis, and editorial opinion. They are often reserved for the Sunday paper, marked off from the rest of the news by a special box or located in the opinion section. In other words, they become "soft news," as opposed to "hard news," as soon as they are written outside of a bureaucratic scheme of relevance which focuses on official dispositions.[5]

Besides the dispositional aspect of cases, another, equally important bureaucratically defined scheme of relevance exists in reporters' work. This is based on an orientation toward policy versus administrative matters in bureaucratic work. The policy-administrative scheme of relevance derives from a fundamental political division of labor in governmental work: legislative or executive bodies deal with (or ought to deal with) policy matters, while an administrative staff deals with (or ought to deal with) administrative matters. Policy matters are considered political decisions (matters of opinion) of widespread importance which provide guidelines for the conduct of bureaucrats (in the form of work instructions to an administrative staff) and the conduct of citizens (in the form of new laws and taxes). Administrative matters are considered technical decisions (matters of professional problem-solving) which are made in the actual implementation of policy decisions.

Bureaucratic work is self-consciously organized in these terms. The policy-administrative distinction is a principle upon which decision-making authority and bureaucratic work are distributed or delegated. As such, it provides participants in bureaucratic settings with procedures for organizing their work. Examples of such procedures are as follows:

1. If the business before us is an administrative matter and this is a policy-making setting, then "rubber-stamp" the matter.

2. If the business before us is a policy question and this is an administrative setting, then refer the matter to a policy-making body.

3. Serious questions about administrative matters should be taken up outside policy-making settings.

Thus, the policy-administrative distinction is used as rational grounds for deciding whether any given matter belongs in (is relevant to) this or that bureaucratic body, and whether it deserves serious consideration or ought to be rubber-stamped.

The distinction between policy and administrative business is so well known around institutions of government that it is normally taken for granted and left as an unnoticed background feature of all governmental work. Both the individuals who produce formal governmental business, in files or in meetings, *and the journalists who cover these files and meetings* employ the distinction as a means for deciding what matters of business are important and what are trivial. The same procedures which organize bureaucratic work and organize the relevance of that work for bureaucrats also are used by reporters to sort out the more newsworthy from the less newsworthy.

For example, on every formal agenda for city and county meetings there were items of business which reporters would know in advance as potentially newsworthy policy matters, while other agenda items were known in advance to be merely administrative matters on the agenda only for technical reasons. I observed that all beat reporters (and not just *Record* journalists) who attended these formal meetings would get agendas days in advance in order to note which would be the potentially newsworthy events. To distinguish newsworthy from trivial items these reporters were relying on the policy-administrative distinction. The actual determination of whether any given agenda item was policy or administrative was an ad hoc decision for reporters, primarily depending on the way the item was presented in the agenda,[6] any previous experience the reporter had with the matter, and the way local officials were talking about it before the formal meeting.

Let us now take up another use of bureaucratic phase structures. What would have happened if Slovekin had not been lucky enough to stumble upon Martha Mungan's hearing and if he had not had a district attorney willing to give him the story (a source which the justice reporter did not routinely rely upon anyway)? This would have been no problem at all. Slovekin simply could have gone to the court clerk's office, located Martha Mungan's case file, and found (in a document called the conditional plea agreement) the essential facts that he learned at the readiness and settlement hearing.

Not only do agency personnel bureaucratically organize and formally stage the transition of a case from one phase to the next, they also record this transition in their files. And they organize these files in ways useful to newsworkers, i.e., in terms of bureaucratically defined phase structures. File folders represent histories of cases (or agenda items), and the contents of records invariably focus on past, present, and future dispositions of the case.

Journalists count on this record-keeping feature of the agencies on their beats and not simply in the event that they miss something they wanted to witness. Quite the contrary: they know that they need not witness everything they write about. They can choose strategically what to view firsthand and what to catch in the files at their leisure. In the following interview segment, the justice reporter Slovekin explained his strategy:

s: [The preliminary hearing, the arraignment, and the readiness and settlement hearing] I can attend in person if I want. Normally I don't. There's just too much going on for me. I might for a murder case, but normally I won't. But I will be aware of the story since I did it, you know, a story when the man was arrested. And if I decided it's the kind of case we'll follow through on, then I can at any given time in the future go to the [master] file in court and see what happened on any of those hearings. It'll be in the file and tell me almost everything I need to know. . . .

mf: [Is the sentencing] the same as the other hearings? You can either go or you can see the disposition of the case [in the master file]?

s: Normally I would prefer to go to a sentencing. . . .

mf: Why?

s: I just—well, because a sentencing is the critical point. It's where the judgment is passed. For one thing the judge can refuse that conditional plea agreement [i.e., plea bargain]. . . . He may have second thoughts 'cause of the probation report. . . . So he has an option, which is almost never exercised. But what if, you know, what if he did that in court and I wasn't there? Or what if the defendant leaped out the window? Uh, it's just simply if you're interested in a case then you ought to be there when the guy is sentenced. (Fishman interview 3-19-74, pp. 6–8.)

Notice that the last phase of the criminal justice phase structure is a critical phase for the reporter. It is not like other phases which can be covered through the files. It represents the ultimate disposition of the case. As such, the reporter tries not to miss this stage in person. The last phase acts as a selection rule for deciding what activities the reporter will attend.

All beat reporters made it a point to attend cases personally at least in their last stage. In fact, because of the unwieldy number of formal meetings constantly happening on his beat, the city hall reporter said that he made it a point to attend only meetings in which issues were likely to receive their final dispositions. He put it this way in explaining which meetings of city commissions he attended:

> The reason that we cover the planning commission as a matter of practice is because their decisions are final unless they're appealed to the city council. . . . Therein lies the difference between covering commissions. The general assumption that I have is that if it's gonna come to the vote of the city council anyway, then you can afford to miss it [at the level of city commissions]. (Fishman interview 12-24-73, pp. 11–12.)

The final dispositional phase not only serves as the reporter's selection rule for attending things like legislative meetings and court hearings. It also serves as a signal to the journalist that this is the last point at which a story can be written about a case. Wieder relates how the justice reporter frequently experienced this process of waiting until the last stage to write a story:

> At first he would tell the city editor what was going on at each of the trials. The city editor typically told him to cover all of them, and then when whatever was happening in one of the trials was boring, or not exciting, or not intriguing with reference to the reporter's sense of news, he would tell the police reporter to hold the material from that trial until the next day or until something interesting happened, or until finally there was a conviction or result. For example, there is a [law suit] going on in which the testimony is regarded by the reporter as boring. He won't write anything until a decision comes through. (Wieder field notes 11-13-64, p. 3.)

Another crucial stage for reporters in phase structures is the first phase. Whereas the last phase signals the reporter's last chance to do a story, the first stage signals the reporter's first chance. It is the official beginning for the publishable career of a story. The journalistic sense of the crucialness of this first event phase is quite strong. A reporter often will not write anything until the case has officially begun its career, even when the reporter knows things are happening on a case but are happening before the first news event phase (e.g., a police investigation, or the actual commission of a crime). I observed instances where a crime was a nonpublishable event for the justice reporter because he learned of it before the police did or before the police had a chance to report an investigation or an arrest. In such cases the reporter would take notes on the officially invisible happening and then wait to publish the information until the police had launched the case into its arrest phase. Thus, a necessary component of crime news is the police. Crime news is primarily news about the actions of the police and the courts, and only secondarily is it news about criminal activities.

Nonevents

We have seen how bureaucratic phase structures serve as schemes of interpretation which define news events. By implication, these schemes also define what activities within the reporter's beat territory are nonevents. Because I have maintained that no complex of activities is inherently an event without someone defining it as such —without someone marking it out of a stream of activity as noteworthy—then how can I speak of something being an event which has not been noticed as such?

To answer this question we need to see that the formulation of an event is always relative to some shared scheme of interpretation. This also means that individuals or groups who, either advertently or inadvertently, do not share the same schemes of interpretation can see different events in the same displays of behavior. A behavioral display from one point of view can be obviously a very significant event, while from another point of view it can either go unnoticed or be noticed but deemed trivial, unnoteworthy, a fragment of something else. Moreover, one can notice that others who were also present did not see an event, i.e., for them it was a nonevent.

A nonevent is something which cannot be seen under a certain scheme of interpretation but can be seen under a different one. Implicitly, the notion of a nonevent includes at least two schemes of interpretation: one which leads an individual to see something, and one which leads an individual not to see something. As such, the concept is relational; it refers to a discontinuity between two perspectives.

I have taken such pains to spell out the concept of a nonevent in order to distinguish it from another notion that is frequently employed in the literature on news bias (Lang and Lang 1953, 1968; White 1964; Gieber 1956, 1964; Östgaard 1965; Robinson 1970). The concept of "news selectivity" is used to explain why some events are reported by journalists and some events are not. Although such explanations are part of my purpose also, I question the assumption contained in the concept of news selectivity that all events (both the reported and the unreported) are objective, unformulated entities "out there" in the newsworld, and that they are "given" in perception and available to any competent, clearheaded observer. Consequently, most sociologists studying news bias have assumed that they (and perhaps a few other select social scientists) are objective enough to recognize all the "really real" events, against which they can measure the extent and pattern of selective reporting by journalists.

News selectivity has its theoretical roots in the concept of selective perception. My notion of nonevents cannot be fitted into that concept, insofar as selective perception is understood to imply some sort of perceptual filter which stands between the knower and a world of pure, unformulated events. Nonevents are not the pure events screened out by selective perception. It makes no sense to speak of pure, unformulated events. Any event arises in the relationship between a knower (employing schemes of interpretation and schemes of relevance) and behaviors in a material world (which are in and of themselves either meaningless or unknowable). Molotch and Lester (1974: 102) summarize this point:

> Our conception is not of a finite set of things that "really happen out there" from which selection is made; our idea is not analogous to selective perception of the physical world. We propose . . . that what is "really happening" is identical with what people attend to.

Selective perception and news selectivity are objectivist, nonrelational concepts which obscure the way in which events are formulated in newswork.

To explicate exactly what nonevents are for journalists, let us look at two rather typical cases in which reporters saw no event, while other persons within the same setting were clearly trying to formulate such an event.

Case 1: The Invisible Crank

In the course of their annual budget hearings, the county board of supervisors were considering next year's budget for the sheriff's department. This item, like all other items of budget business, followed a prescribed sequence: first the chief administrative officer and the auditor-controller read their recommendations, then the board questioned the two bureaucrats, the floor was then open for opponents and proponents to step up to the public podium, and finally the supervisors debated and voted on the issue.

During the public input phase (as it is called in those meetings), the speeches centered around whether the administrator was justified in recommending fewer new deputy sheriff positions than the county sheriff had asked for. The top officials of the sheriff's department were arguing for a larger force to keep the present service ratio (the number of patrolmen per 1,000 inhabitants) in line with population increases. Two of the supervisors and one of the official taxpayers' groups argued that the extra positions were not needed if one calculated the service ratio in a somewhat different way.

During this debate a young woman stepped up to the podium, introduced herself, and said that she felt any consideration of funding the sheriff's department was shameful. She then recounted an incident involving her and sheriff's deputies in the community of Pacific Point. She had been selling wares from a pushcart in the street when a sheriff's car pulled up to her. Two deputies stepped out and asked what she was doing and if she had a license. She answered that she had no license, but that she didn't know she needed one. At this point in the story the chairman of the board of supervisors interrupted, asking the woman to come to her point or to give up the floor. The woman simply continued with her story.

She said the officers told her to get into the patrol car, and when she refused she was handcuffed and pulled in. When she insisted on knowing why she was being accosted, she was subjected to verbal abuse. At the sheriff's station she was bound hand and foot and left in a room for several hours. Once again, the chairman interrupted and asked the woman to leave the podium, but she continued the account. She said that she was finally released with no explanation. On several occasions after this incident she tried to lodge a complaint with the sheriff's department, but it was never accepted. By this point in her presentation the woman was extremely upset. She berated the behavior of the county sheriffs as less than human, as incomprehensible. Again, the chairman broke in, telling the woman that they had heard enough and, if she insisted on remaining at the podium, she would be removed. The woman quietly left.

From the point of view of those present the woman's talk was so out of character with the budget proceedings that her presentation was bizarre. She was just another crank. Throughout the woman's speech no one in the room would maintain eye contact with her; some people showed their uninvolvement by doodling, reading, conversing with others; others clearly indicated their impatience by rolling their eyes, smiling, sighing, making jokes. At the press table all four reporters acted as if the woman's talk signaled a time out. Reporters put down their pencils and stopped taking notes. One journalist left the room for awhile; others started up conversations about matters other than what was happening in the meeting at that moment. Reporters' attention on the meeting returned as soon as the woman left the podium.

Needless to say, this incident was never reported in any news medium in Purissima. It was a nonevent, not in the sense that it was never seen but in the sense that journalists considered it not worth seeing. It never occurred to reporters that it could be a newsworthy event. It could only be an uncomfortable time out, a snag in the flow of the meeting. Why?

After all, the speaker was not incoherent, nor was her argument, when taken on its own terms, senseless or irrelevant. But instead of speaking to the issues of service ratios, tax cuts, and how many sheriff positions to allocate, this woman talked about a corrupt law enforcement agency unworthy of any public support. The course of action she proposed, however, was seen as unreasonable because it was not one among the set of alternatives procedurally prescribed for the board to entertain in budget hearings. Moreover, the woman was not (and made no pretense to be) speaking from a structural position of interest: she represented no formally constituted group which fit into the constellation of interests appropriate to the issue.

To entertain her talk as appropriate to the occasion, those present would have had to break the procedural bounds of the budget session in order to take on a wider political perspective from which one could see as problematic the issue of any funding for the sheriff's department.

Case 2: The Invisible Controversy

At a Purissima city council meeting a routine agenda item came up entitled: "Recommendation for contract award: Bid No. 943—one three-wheeled street sweeper, diesel powered, to lowest bidder, Boulder Beach Machine Co., in total amount of $17,623.20." The item was placed on the agenda by Public Works Director Dennis Dolan. Matters of this sort, in which a department head requests approval to purchase equipment after competitive bidding, are normally rubber-stamped by the council.

A council member began by pointedly asking Dolan why he was replacing the old gasoline street sweeper with a more expensive ($2,000 more) diesel-powered vehicle. Dolan said that the more expensive street sweeper would last longer and consume less fuel. Two other council members, however, joined in to press the original objection that there was no need for more expensive equipment. This time they also seemed to be implying that "something was funny," that the public works director's motives were suspect. A controversy quickly took shape, with three council members defending Dolan's street sweeper, three questioning it, and one refraining from debate. It was apparent to the four reporters at the press table and to others present that this was not merely a dispute over a street sweeper. One side was implying that something was defective in Dolan's decision (indicating incompetence or venality on his part); the other side was asserting that this whole matter was being overblown, that it was not the business of the council to embroil itself in the details of staff operations, and that the council should show trust in its department heads in administrative matters. After twenty minutes of increasingly bitter debate, the council voted four to three that Dolan should return next week with more information.

While all this was going on, the four members of the press (including the *Record*'s city hall reporter) were showing increasing signs of impatience with the controversy. At first the reporters stopped taking notes; then they began showing their disapproval to each other; finally, they were making derisive jokes about the foolishness of the debate. No evidence could be found in their comments that they considered the controversy anything other than a stupid debate over a trivial matter unworthy of the time and energy the council put into it.

This incident did not go entirely unreported; the *Record*'s city hall reporter gave it a brief mention in his next day's stories on the council meeting. It was placed, however, toward the end of a long story which cited several miscellaneous items of council business: "In other matters . . . the City Council voted 4–3 to continue until next week the recommendation of Public Works Director R. D. Dolan to purchase a diesel-powered street sweeper." Never was there any mention of the lengthy, bitter dispute preceding the vote. Not only was the controversy invisible in this one-sentence report, but a reader of the story who had not been present at the meeting or who was not an experienced council-watcher and *Record* news reader would not have known why this particular agenda item was reported among all the other routine business transacted that day.[7]

Even though at the time of the incident I was sitting at the press table (as a reporter) making derisive comments about the foolishness of the council along with other journalists, it occurred to me later how this controversy could be seen as an important event in city hall. The controversy dealt explicitly with whether it was appropriate for the council to embroil itself in the details of its staff's administrative decisions. That is, this controversy rendered problematic the policy-administrative scheme of relevance discussed earlier. The street sweeper debate turned into a controversy over whether the council was going to abide by that traditional distinction, trust its public works director, and as a general matter leave the city staff free to make the merely technical decisions. But three of the council members challenged the underlying political analysis of government embodied in the policy-administrative distinction: that power is held by elected, policy-making officials who, in turn, delegate power to a professional staff to implement their decisions. Such an analysis contrasts with alternative political views that power is held by an economic elite which manipulates official decision making, or that power is held by bureaucrats and technicians who form a technocracy which runs government. By reference to these alternative schemes, I could see the debate as significant, relevant, and newsworthy.

But the controversy was a nonevent for the newsworkers at the press table. The incident was not newsworthy material; it was, rather, deemed foolish and a waste of time, because it was an administrative matter which ought to have been rubber-stamped. It prevented other supposedly more revelant policy matters on the agenda from being considered. In short, the controversy was invisible to reporters as a sign of the council's brewing dissatisfaction over who, in fact, was running city government (elected council members or technocrats). And this was invisible because the means by which reporters oriented to the meeting in order to sort out the important from the trivial was also the very topic of the controversy. Most of the debate centered on whether the council members were justified in continually embroiling themselves in administrative detail. For the journalists to have taken this as a serious issue would have meant calling into question a basic procedure for interpreting the beat. Newsworkers do not readily part with their familiar methods of event detection[8]—methods which make coverage of the beat territory possible in the first place.

In an interview several weeks before the street sweeper controversy, the city hall reporter confirmed that as a general matter he ignored these kinds of debates:

I really, sometimes I have to differentiate between the city council as a, uh, policy-making body, and as a body that is involved in administration. I mean there are many things that are strictly administrative, that I think the council doesn't understand are administrative, that are brought to them by [the city's chief administrative officer] as a courtesy. And I don't waste a heck of a lot of time worrying about how the council feels about a situation like that. Sometimes by their very lack of understanding they get involved in a situation that is, uh—so they spend an awful lot of time. Some are a waste of time discussing things that are a cut-and-dried routine administrative matter. (Fishman interview 12-24-73, pp. 6–7.)

The city hall reporter is describing not only the policy-administrative distinction, he is telling us how he uses that distinction in orienting to the activities of the city council. He won't "waste a heck of a lot of time" covering the council's deliberation over administrative matters which "really" belong in the domain of the city staff. For the reporter, only bureaucrats are in a position to know, say, and do newsworthy things about administrative matters, and only council members are in a position to know, say, and do newsworthy things about policy matters.

At this point we can see a good deal of similarity between the two cases I have described. In both nonevents the reporters noticed things going on but ignored them by taking a time out and pointedly showing their disapproval of the activities. Even though they literally saw something, all that they saw in it was a moral character: these were occurrences that did not deserve reporting, that were a waste of everybody's time. These incidents were unnewsworthy in the strongest sense. It is not that the journalists weighed their relative newsworthiness against other events and then rejected the nonevents as not newsworthy enough. Rather, the two incidents were events that never had a chance. As soon as they were encountered the reporters knew to cease paying attention to them as serious material for their news stories. They were unpublishable because they were illegitimate events, incidents which did not belong as topics in the territory (setting) in which they occurred. They did not deserve to be dignified by being published.[9] To publish an illegitimate event would be unprofessional. If the city council became embroiled in a dispute over an administrative matter, it would be misleading to cover this as if it were a policy matter (i.e., report it as a controversy). If a speaker at the county budget hearings condemned the sheriff's department and argued it deserves no public support, it would be misleading to cover this as if it were another plausible argument in the debate. In short, to the reporter nonevents have the quality of being morally seen but professionally unnoticed.[10]

In both of these nonevents, their morally seen and professionally unnoticed character derived from the fact that they were occurrences which stood outside the alternative courses of action procedurally provided for in the bureaucratic setting. Bureaucratic procedures organize activities within formal settings. To follow these activities—to understand what's happening and what's important— reporters rely on these same procedures as schemes of interpretation and schemes of relevance. Incidents which defy, ignore, or question the procedural foundation of the setting, if taken seriously by journalists (i.e., entertained as potential newsworthy events), would bring them to question the very methods they have come to rely upon in doing their work. Nonevents are possible because, ironically, reporters are blinded by their own methods for detecting events.

In nonevents we can see most clearly the tightness of the bond between news events and bureaucratic events. Nonevents are violations of the bureaucratic procedures which organize beat settings. If from a bureaucratic point of view it is not a legitimate occurrence within the setting, then from a journalistic point of view it cannot be a genuine news event.

As I have portrayed it here, the phenomenon of news selectivity at the level of the reporter on the beat is not so much the result of reporters' personal biases or of their attempts to protect friendly bureaucratic sources, or of their following orders from politically motivated editors. Rather, news selectivity is a consequence of journalists' protecting their own methods of event detection—methods which are tightly wedded to the bureaucrat's methods of formulating events.

4. Grounds for Investigating the News

Reporters are held accountable by editors, fellow reporters, and newspaper readers that what they write is not fictitious, fanciful, or one-sided.[1] They are expected to be factually correct (even when the issue of what's going on may be unclear). Thus, once reporters have detected a potential piece of news, they face the question: How do I know this is so? How do I know that this is really what is happening?

To answer this question reporters may or may not do investigative work. For the most part, the potential news that reporters detect comes in the form of other people's accounts: arguments of a defense lawyer in court, information on police arrest reports, statements of a city council member, or tips passed to the reporter by an informant. My concern in this chapter is to describe and explain under what conditions reporters will treat these accounts as fact requiring no investigative work, and under what conditions they feel the need to do further investigative work. In the next chapter I will be concerned with what happens once reporters do feel called upon to do further investigation. There I will describe reporters' methods of investigative work—methods undertaken for a variety of purposes: to substantiate someone's claim as fact, to present all sides of a controversy, or simply to find out more details for a story. Both chapters explore the routine measures reporters take to satisfy themselves, their editors, and potential critics that what they report are the facts. In this process we shall see how the news story itself is formulated.

"Fact" and Bureaucratic Accounts

Whenever journalists did no investigative work on stories (beyond the initial detection of those stories), I found that a single circumstance prevailed in their newswork: the accounts reporters treated as factual, requiring no further investigation or substantiation, were bureaucratic accounts. Typically, these were documents in agency files, officials speaking "on the record," or formally organized activities in meetings. This is not to say that all bureaucratic accounts were taken as factual. But it is to say that the only accounts that were taken at their face value were bureaucratically organized and produced.

The following incident was typical of a noninvestigative piece of newswork. At 7:45 AM the justice reporter, Gene Slovekin, was in the last stages of his work at the sheriff's headquarters. While leafing through the county coroner's reports, Slovekin spotted one document that interested him. It concerned the death of a man who Slovekin guessed was a skid row bum, judging from his place of residence. The man had died on a Greyhound bus enroute to Purissima. As he read through the report, Slovekin took these notes on a slip of paper:

John Henry Truttwell
9–8–23
2250 mon.
23 W. Pelly St.
Centerville—
fell forward in Quintoville
someone tried m–m
went to P
Laguna Perdida dead

I asked Slovekin what these notes meant. He explained these were the "essential facts" of the story: The man's name was John Henry Truttwell. He was born September 8, 1923, and he died at "2250 mon." (10:50 PM the day before). His address was 23 W. Pelly St. The Greyhound originated in Centerville. When it was passing through Quintoville, Truttwell fell forward. A passenger on the bus tried mouth-to-mouth resuscitation ("m–m"). The bus proceeded on to Purissima ("went to P"), but the man was pronounced dead at Laguna Perdida Hospital ("Laguna Perdida dead").

When Slovekin returned to his desk in the newsroom he typed up a short (three column–inch) story from these notes. The story as he typed it and as it appeared on the second page of the local news section of that day's newspaper, read as follows:

MAN, 50, DIES DURING BUS TRIP

A man collapsed and died last night on a Greyhound bus traveling from Centerville to Purissima.

He was identified as John Henry Truttwell, 50, whose last known address was 23 W. Pelly St.

Fellow passengers told police that Truttwell fell forward when the bus was traveling through Quintoville. A woman applied mouth-to-mouth revival efforts while the bus continued here, but Truttwell was dead on arrival at Laguna Perdida Hospital.

What interests us most about this case is that the reporter treated the central element of this story—the man's death on the bus—as a simple fact, and he did so on the basis of a single account, the coroner's document. Slovekin was willing to take it on faith that whoever filled out the coroner's report had accurately recorded a true event.

Notice that there are at least four levels of interlocking accounts here: (1) the accounts of the bus passengers and hospital personnel, (2) the account of these accounts written up by the investigating police on the scene, (3) the account of the police account produced by the clerk who filled out the coroner's report, and (4) the account of the coroner's report written as a news story by the justice reporter. The most salient feature of this chain of accounts is that each succeeding report is based on its immediately preceding report, which is not necessarily the original activity or the original account of that activity. The reporter's news story is wholly an account of an account of an account of an account. As a matter of course, Slovekin did not bother to confirm any of the information in the coroner's report by verifying the first-level accounts: he did not interview bus passengers or hospital personnel to see if their stories coincided with and corroborated the coroner's story; and he did not examine the dead man in the morgue to see if he was in fact there, in fact dead, and in fact a man. Moreover, Slovekin trusted that the bureaucratic record-keeping apparatus honestly and faithfully recorded the accounts offered by the bus passengers and hospital personnel (in the police field report) and the account offered by the investigating police (in the coroner's report).

This typical case of straight news reporting indicates that bureaucratic "facts" are the hard data of newswork. Conversely, nonbureaucratic accounts are soft data, unconfirmed reports, or speculation. Without further investigation they cannot be published as hard news. An important consequence of this is that the journalist's own inferences from bureaucratic accounts (or any other accounts for that matter) cannot be reported without further investigation. Recall that Slovekin suspected the man who died on the bus was a skid row bum. He inferred this from the man's last-known address (and perhaps his age and sex) on the coroner's report. Yet this inference remained unpublished speculation because Slovekin never bothered to investigate it. On the other hand, Slovekin treated the dead man's name, age, and address as publishable facts, even though these too must have been inferred by someone, i.e., the investigating police on the scene inferred a dead man carrying a social security card with the name John Henry Truttwell must be, in fact, John Henry Truttwell. Who made such inferences and how they were made did not seem to concern the reporter. All that mattered was that they appeared as fact on the coroner's report. If reporters draw their own inferences from available accounts, they cannot report them as facts. If somebody else draws the inferences—and usually this someone else is an official empowered to do so—then the journalist can treat these inferences as hard facts.

The fact that reporters are restricted from drawing their own (nonbureaucratically substantiated) inferences in hard news stories often means that they cannot come out and say what they mean to say or would like to say. They privately talk about, but publicly will not write about, things they know to be true because in print such things would look like biased journalism. For example, Crouse (1974: 270–271) relates an incident in which *New York Times* political reporter Robert Semple felt it necessary to stop short of making the central point he meant to make in a series of news stories about Richard Nixon's conduct during the 1972 Nixon-McGovern presidential campaign. Crouse begins by quoting one of Semple's stories appearing in the September 28, 1972, *New York Times*:

The President discussed neither his programs nor his opponent's in detail. Instead, he employed broad strokes to paint the South Dakotan as a willing captive of the left who had isolated himself from Mr. Nixon's vision of the American temperament.

But not once did Semple write that Nixon had *wrongly* accused Mc-Govern of wanting to confiscate wealth and weaken the country militarily. In effect, his stories said that Nixon had begun to use strong rhetoric and had thrown some tough accusations at McGovern, but then McGovern was doing the same thing to Nixon. We talked about the stories while he was writing them, and at one point Semple said: "You can say that Nixon's attack on McGovern was couched in severe language and general terms, but you can't then write—'and bore no resemblance to what McGovern has been saying.' "[11]

Reporters' freedom to report inferences, hunches, and theories of what's going on which stem from nonbureaucratic sources (i.e., from journalists themselves or from some "unauthorized" informant)—and to report these without doing further investigative work—is generally quite limited in the American news media. The extent of freedom from straight reporting varies from news organization to news organization and primarily depends on the emerging editorial policy within each organization. Because for journalists this issue is explicitly a matter of editorial policy, reporters and editors often lock horns over their paper's policy. Usually these battles erupt over particular stories that editors consider too speculative and opinionated and that reporters consider necessarily interpretive and analytic.[2] Crouse (1974: 115–116) relates such an incident between political reporter Jules Witcover and his editors on the Los Angeles *Times* during the 1972 presidential campaign.

So Witcover kept writing meticulously fair analysis stories, and the *Times* kept balking. The biggest showdown came at the end of September over a story on Nixon's non-campaign. As the weeks went by and Nixon kept refusing to face the public, Witcover knew that he would have to write a story about it, pointing out the injustice of a one-candidate campaign. After all, he had slapped McGovern for trying to avoid newsmen. But he kept putting the article off, waiting for a news "hook" that would allow him to write that story in a way that wouldn't offend the *Times*. Finally, at the end of September, McGovern solved the problem for him. Addressing a conference of UPI editors, McGovern accused the press of failing to meet its responsibilities by not forcing Nixon to answer questions on the issues. . . .

So Witcover began his story by quoting McGovern's accusations. While McGovern's argument was self-serving, wrote Witcover, it did point up a serious problem: How could the press provide balanced coverage when only one candidate was campaigning? Of course, Witcover went on, the President did have some legitimate reasons for not campaigning. . . .

But then Witcover pointed out the dangers of a lopsided campaign. The public needed a chance to see both candidates questioned on the issues. When only one man campaigned the whole system was undermined.

Finally, Witcover concluded that although the President might have real reasons for not going out on the stump, he could still hold a press conference . . . and answer political questions, something the President had refused to do at the few news conferences he had held earlier in the year. . . .

The editors in Los Angeles killed the story. They told Witcover that it didn't "come off" and that it was an "opinion" story. Witcover couldn't believe it. He felt that the story was a classic example of the difference between analysis and opinion. He has marshaled all the facts, and drawn his conclusion solely from them. But the editors couldn't see it. Witcover, who was covering McGovern in New York, had long arguments with them over Long Distance. The solution was simple, they told him. All he had to do was get other people to make the same points and draw the same conclusion and then write the article *in their words*. Yes, said Witcover, but that was *reporting*, not *analysis*. . . . The editors asked him to do it over. He refused.

The most extreme and well-known example of news organizations holding to a consistent policy of straight reporting are the American wire services, the Associated Press (AP) and United Press International (UPI). Shortly after the AP was established in 1848, its Washington bureau chief flatly stated its organizational policy:

My business is to communicate facts. My instructions do not allow me to make any comment upon the facts which I communicate. My dispatches are merely dry matters of fact and detail (quoted in Hudson 1873: 732).

Since that time wire service reporting has barely budged from this policy:

Wire stories are usually bland, dry and overly cautious. There is an inverse proportion between the number of persons a reporter reaches and the amount he can say. The larger the audience, the more inoffensive and inconclusive the article must be. Many of the wire men are repositories of information they can never write about. Pye Chamberlin, a young UPI reporter . . . [is] an expert on the Dark Side of Congress. He could tell you about a prominent Senator's battle to overcome his addiction to speed, or about Humphrey's habit of popping twenty-five One-A-Day Vitamins with a shot of bourbon when he needed some fast energy. But Pye couldn't tell his audience (Crouse 1974: 20).

Not all news organizations adhere this consistently to a policy of straight reporting. But the fact that the wire services do is highly consequential for all U.S. media, especially newspapers. Virtually every one of America's 1,750 daily newspapers use the AP, UPI, or both. With the exception of the few large metropolitan dailies that maintain state, national, and international bureaus, American newspapers—including the Purissima *Record*—exclusively rely on the wire services for all but local news. Even on the few papers which maintain their own bureaus, wire service reports almost always arrive in the newsroom first, and editors often gauge their own reporters' stories against expectations that wire services have aroused (Crouse 1974: 19–20).

News organizations which maintain a less rigid policy toward straight reporting usually limit their softer news stories within certain bounds: the Sunday edition of the paper, specially labeled and demarcated columns and boxes, and so forth. This was the policy of the Purissima *Record* and is apparently the policy of most newspapers. Some large metropolitan dailies maintain a somewhat looser policy of containment toward interpretive reports: *The Christian Science Monitor* generally encourages interpretive reporting, while the *New York Times* and Washington *Post* selectively encourage it on certain topics at certain times (e.g., the *Post*'s and *Times*' 1973 Watergate coverage and the *Times*' 1975 Indochina coverage). The only large-scale news organizations, aside from *The Christian Science Monitor*, which consistently produce interpretive reports, i.e., which lie at the other extreme from the policy of the wire services, are not newspapers but weekly news magazines such as *Time* and *Newsweek*.

Whichever way editorial policy falls on this issue—and it usually falls on the side of straight reporting—the standards of news fact remain unchanged. Information which is bureaucratically organized, produced, and provided is hard fact; it is the stuff that makes up straight reporting. Any other kind of information (not subjected to further investigation) does not have the character of hard fact; it is the stuff that makes up interpretive reports or news analyses. Reporters and editors may disagree on how much news analysis belongs in a newspaper, but they do not question the validity of the distinction between news analysis and straight reporting. They do not question the assumption that bureaucratically produced accounts are somehow harder data than nonbureaucratically inferred information. Journalists routinely will doubt in a *global* sense nonbureaucratic accounts. But they will not entertain this kind of doubt when faced with official accounts. As we shall see, it takes special motives to doubt bureaucratic accounts.

To understand why this is so we need to examine the journalist's general criterion of facticity. This fundamental principle of news fact can be stated like this: *something is so because somebody says it*. Newsworkers take their facts from other people's accounts. Unlike social scientists, reporters rarely gather data by conducting large-scale surveys, running laboratory experiments, or engaging in participant observation. Unlike detectives, reporters rarely sift through physical evidence or run tests on it. Instead reporters will talk to people (including social scientists and detectives) and treat their accounts as fact.[3] As we shall see, this means that the journalist's investigative methods are primarily interview methods. Incidentally, note the economy of the principle "something is so because somebody says it." On the one hand, it frees newsworkers from determining facts by using the sophisticated, expensive, or time-consuming methods of other kinds of investigators. On the other hand, the principle allows newsworkers to capitalize on the fruits of these more complex techniques by talking with those who have already used them.

But this formulation of the principle of facticity is not yet complete. "Something is so because somebody says it" does not mean that the "somebody" saying something can be just anybody. Rather, it must be somebody in a position to know what they say, somebody entitled to know what they say. No newspaper fact can be asserted independently of some competent knower or observer. The assumed competence of the news source is the matter of concern for reporters and not necessarily the procedures whereby the news source (or the reporter) arrives at the assertion.[4]

Typically, competent knowers for journalists are bureaucrats and agency officials. I showed in Chapters 2 and 3 that reporters see and treat the world as bureaucratically organized. As Berger and co-authors (1973: 43–44) point out, this kind of bureaucratic consciousness includes the idea that specific bureaucrats are competent knowers of specific things:

A key notion in the individual's knowledge of the bureaucratic system is that of *competence*: each jurisdiction and each agency within it is competent only for its assigned sphere of life and is supposed to have expert knowledge appropriate to its sphere.

Bureaucrats are seen as competent knowers by virtue of their social structural position, i.e., their official assignment over a jurisdiction. Thus, they have a social warrant, they are entitled or authorized, to know certain things.

Consider the following *New York Times* front page story about the "uncertain evacuation" of six hundred foreign refugees from Phnom Penh, Cambodia:[5]

---

600 FOREIGNERS HELD IN CAMBODIA REACH THAILAND
30 Miles, Cambodians Said
by DAVID A. ANDELMAN

ARANYAPRATHET, May 2 [1975] —Cambodian Communist soldiers had told the special envoy of the President of France here earlier today that the foreigners held for more than two weeks in the French Embassy in Phnom Penh were about 30 miles from the Thai-Cambodian border. However, the soldiers did not explain what caused the delay in getting to the frontier here.

Ambassador-at-Large Marc Bonnefous, sent here yesterday by President Valery Giscard d'Estaing, met for about 10 minutes earlier with about two dozen Cambodian troops across the barbed wire strung over the narrow wooden bridge that is the only road link between the two nations.

As he walked from the bridge, which spans a small stream, Mr. Bonnefous told reporters on this side that the soldiers "are saying that our compatriots are about 55 kilometers from the border."

"But," he went on, "they say, 'We have problems.' I am not very optimistic on the refugees coming in tomorrow." Also, he said, he did not know whether all 610 evacuees would arrive together.

Mr. Bonnefous said that the head of the Cambodian delegation today had been the "head of the Cambodian frontier region." But Chhay Born Lay, the Cambodian interpreter, who is a newsman for the Associated Press, said later that the Communist spokesman was apparently only a sergeant in charge of the border-patrol unit.

And so there was no firm proof today that the foreigners were, in fact, about 30 miles from the frontier, nor was there any word whether that group included all of those who took refuge in the Phnom Penh embassy.

For two days, Cambodian soldiers have been saying across the barbed wire that the foreigners are "nearing." They have advanced several explanations for the delay: Bridges washed out or bombed out; lack of gasoline for the vehicles, of which, Mr. Bonnefous said, he "understood from Paris" there were four. None of this has been confirmed. . . .

The reporter makes it clear in this story that the Cambodian accounts of the refugees' whereabouts and safety are doubtful because the sources—the Cambodian soldiers and their leader—were not seen as having bureaucratic and jurisdictional competence over this information. Regardless of the procedures whereby the soldiers came to know what they said, they were not recognized as being in an official position to know what they said. For reporters, the most credible information or the hardest data are accounts which come from the "most competent" news sources, who, in turn, are bureaucrats and officials recognized as having jurisdiction over the events in question. Bureaucratic hierarchies constitute "hierarchies of credibility" (Becker 1967) for journalists.[6]

Reasons for Believing Bureaucratic Accounts

So it appears that journalists are predisposed to believe that bureaucratic accounts represent the facts of a case. There are two important reasons for this. One has to do with the socially sanctioned character of bureaucrats' competence to know, and the other has to do with what I shall call the "performative" character of bureaucratic accounts. Let us first take up the sanctioning aspect of bureaucratic knowledge.

Journalists not only see certain agency officials as having a special vantage point from which they can observe events,[7] but they also see officials as socially authorized and socially sanctioned knowers. This means several things:

1. Journalists believe that bureaucrats are not only in a position to know certain things but that these officials ought to know what they are in a position to know. Journalists do not simply hold the attitude, "If anyone knows X, then such-and-such official will know it." They also believe, ". . . and even if officials do not know it, they should know it." Like others in the society who grant officials the legitimacy of their position, newsworkers hold officials responsible for knowing what it is their job to know. This expectation has two corollary expectations.

2. Newsworkers believe that when officials show that they do not know what they should know, then journalists ought to hold officials responsible to know it. In short, officials can be negatively sanctioned for not doing their job. Journalists feel they are justified, if not obliged, to do such sanctioning because "the public has a right to know," and the press, as self-appointed representative of the public, has a duty to look out for the public interest. As the following incident shows, this sanctioning may consist of nothing more than complaining about official incompetence to the nearest listener (in this case, the researcher). The incident occurred while the justice reporter was at Purissima's civil defense center covering a major flood in the area.

The head of the local civil defense [office] came out to talk to the reporter. The reporter had never met him before. The man explained that he was acting as public information officer. . . . The reporter asked him what action they were taking, where the flooding was, how many vehicles they had out, how many men they had out, and where the sandbags could be obtained and what citizens should do to get sandbags. After we left, the reporter said, "These official bureaucrats sure don't stay on the ball and know what they should." His complaint was that for many of the questions . . . the head of the local civil defense had no answers: he didn't know how many men were out in the field; he only guessed and didn't know exactly how many vehicles they had nor even where all the trouble points were. I asked the reporter why this official should know. . . . His answer . . . was, "The public needs to know." (Wieder field notes 11-10-64, p. 4.)

Sanctions can take stronger forms: journalists may complain to higher officials in the offending agency, or, on occasion, they may write about "official incompetence" in their news stories.

3. Newsworkers believe that when officials show that, in fact, they know what they should know, then officials ought to be recognized as knowing it and not merely recognized as offering just another version of events. When someone who ought to know the facts also claims to know the facts, then journalists treat that person's claim as more than just a claim. Just as journalists negatively sanction officials who do not know what they should, they positively sanction officials who do know what they should by reporting the official's account as "the facts."

In short, newsworkers are predisposed to treat bureaucratic accounts as factual because journalists participate in upholding a normative order of authorized knowers in the society. Significantly, the newsworker's participation in this normative order is not simply a matter of belief; it is also a position of convenience. To do their work journalists need competent knowers. The journalist holds officials responsible for knowing what it is their job to know *because* of the newsworker's own need for news. For this reason, reporters notice official incompetence when bureaucrats cannot give them the information they need. Thus, the reporter's perception of bureaucratic incompetence stems not from officials' inability to get their job done but from their inability to make news for the reporter.

The second major reason for journalists' acceptance of bureaucratic accounts as statements of true facts and events has to do with a particular feature of those accounts—a feature I will refer to as their "performative" character. In 1955 the English philosopher of language, J. L. Austin, coined the term "performative" to refer to certain kinds of linguistic utterances which do something rather than merely say something (Austin 1961: 222). Statements or propositions assert something about the world; they can be true or false.

The performative utterance, by contrast, can never be either [true or false]: it has its own special job, it is used to perform an action. To issue such an utterance *is* to perform the action. . . . Here are some examples:
 I name this ship Liberté.
 I apologize.
 I welcome you.
 I advise you to do it (Austin 1971: 13).

Performatives cannot be true or false because they are things in themselves and not statements about things. However, performatives can be invalid when they are not done correctly:

The performative must be issued in a situation appropriate in all respects for the act in question: if the speaker is not in the conditions required for its performance (and there are many such occasions), then his utterance will be . . . "unhappy" [i.e., invalid, meaningless, hollow, bizarre, etc.] (Austin 1971: 14).

 Imagine a man getting angry at his wife for driving poorly, taking her driver's license away, and sending it to the department of motor vehicles with a note saying he has just revoked her license. The letter from the man revoking his wife's license is what Austin would call an "unhappy" performative. It wouldn't work: the performative (the letter) meant to revoke the license could only be seen as an absurdity by the bureaucrat who opened the letter. The circumstances surrounding the linguistic act (the letter) were inappropriate: husbands are not authorized persons when it comes to revoking driver's licenses, and the procedure followed in this case did not involve the proper channels. Anybody in the society should know that driver's licenses can be revoked only by judges in court proceedings and that the court is only one of a number of agencies who process the case before it reaches the files of the department of motor vehicles.

 As can be seen from this example, bureaucracies are fertile grounds for performatives. Bureaucracies are established and maintained precisely for the purpose of constituting the socially appropriate circumstances under which a variety of public acts can be accomplished successfully: the certification of births, deaths, and marriages; the granting of privileges to vote, drive, and buy guns; the enforcement of obligations to pay taxes, serve on juries, and obey laws; and countless other things. For the most part such acts are performatives in the sense that they are accomplished by the use of language under socially appropriate (bureaucratic) circumstances. Bureaucratic performatives occur both in situated social interactions (e.g., city council meetings) and in documents (e.g., official contracts recording negotiated pleas). Here I focus mainly on bureaucratic documents to discuss the performative character of bureaucratic accounts because this characteristic can be seen most clearly in documents and because reporters rely heavily on such documents as sources of hard facts.

Consider a document like the conditional plea agreement. This is an official form filled out and signed by a defendant, the defendant's lawyer, the district attorney, and the judge after all parties have negotiated and agreed upon a reduction of criminal charges in exchange for a guilty plea. At first glance such a document appears to describe or report an event (the plea bargain). But it is far more; the document is a central part of the event itself. The plea bargaining session is organized around producing such a document, and the interaction during the session continually orients toward what the document will stipulate once it is drawn up and signed. However, after the negotiations are completed, for all practical (organizational) purposes, the document comes to embody the plea bargain event, while the actual interactions which produced the document are obscured or lost.

Many other kinds of bureaucratic records are performatives in the full sense that conditional plea agreements are. Wills, leases, insurance policies, land transfers, work contracts, patents, deeds, and bank accounts are all events made concrete in a document, or documents which constitute an event. A will *is* the bequeathing of an estate; a lease *is* the leasing of property; an insurance policy *is* the insuring of valuables.

It is not hard to see, then, why reporters are inclined to believe what they read in performative documents. How could things be other than what these documents say they are? A conditional plea agreement cannot incorrectly describe a plea bargain because it *is* the plea bargain. As long as it is a valid document, what it says is what has to be. Journalists love performative documents because these are the hardest facts they can get their hands on.

Things have to be the way they are stated in performative documents in the sense that newsworkers and others in the society count on the fact that the information in the document is, and will continue to be, normatively enforced in the society. For example, the terms of a negotiated plea as they appear in the conditional plea agreement are guaranteed to be true by the normal operations of a criminal justice system whose personnel are socially sanctioned to act on the basis of the terms just as they appear in the conditional plea agreement. To the extent that information in bureaucratic records must be the basis for further inference and action on a case, that information has an enforced factual character and that document has the quality of being a performative.

What I am implying here, though, is that the performative or enforced factual character of bureaucratic accounts is a matter of degree. Some documents are more performative than others. Within any single document, the performative character is uneven or spotty; it only guarantees the factual character of some, but not all, of the information in the document. Thus, while an arrest report can never incorrectly describe the fact of an arrest or the charges for which the person was arrested, it can incorrectly describe the suspect's address or the circumstances that led to the arrest. This possibility for error is quite important for the workings of the criminal justice system because otherwise there would be no point in the case going to court for the determination of such matters.

The normal operations of the criminal justice system guarantee that there is no possibility for error in parts of the arrest report (e.g., the fact of the arrest and its charges). If there is an arrest report but no suspect arrested, a legal arrest could not have been made; conversely, if an arrest has been made, but there is no report of it, then there is no legal arrest. To use another example, a deed to a piece of land lacks a performative character only to the extent that ownership (or the terms of ownership) of that land is decided upon any basis other than what the deed specifies.

In short, the basis of facticity in the society (and not just facticity for journalists) is its expected enforcement. Information which can be counted upon to be the basis for further inference and action by untold others is information which is treated as factual and, thus, which is made factual for all practical purposes. As this suggests, it is not just journalists for whom bureaucratic documents are hard facts. Early in the history of modern sociology, Emile Durkheim (and those in the field of moral statistics in general) directed sociologists to bureaucracies for their hard data and social facts. Lawyers, social workers, doctors, bankers, detectives, probation and parole officers, and bureaucrats in a variety of agencies rely upon bureaucratic documents from a variety of *other* agencies to provide hard facts.

For example, Zimmerman (1974: 128–143) found this same phenomenon operating among social workers in a welfare agency. As a routine and sanctioned procedure for verifying the eligibility of applicants, social workers relied upon bureaucratic documents from other agencies as providing hard facts: to verify the welfare applicant's intention to find employment, social workers would call agencies where the applicant allegedly sought employment, and the worker would ask if the agency had any record of an application for employment. Such a record constituted factual evidence of intention to be employed. To verify welfare applicants' claims as to how much money they had saved, the social worker would call their bank and, again, take the bank's accounting of their savings as plain fact. Zimmerman (1974: 132–133) notes that, as a routine part of their work, agency personnel from the outset saw official documents as reliable and applicants' claims as open to doubt.

Doubting Bureaucratic Accounts

I have shown two reasons why newsworkers are predisposed to accept bureaucratic accounts as factual. First, some (but not all) bureaucratic accounts have a performative character. They are accounts which *are* what they report. They have a factual character guaranteed by the normal operations of the society within which they are produced and of which they are a part. When journalists see performative accounts, they know they have seen hard facts.

Second, all bureaucratic accounts—even if they are not performative—are from the outset credible accounts because journalists subscribe to the belief that officials ought to know what they are in a position to know. When newsworkers see a bureaucratic account which displays such expected knowledge, they will not treat it as just another version of events because it has not come from just another knower. It is a credible account because it is produced by a competent source—a competence which is socially sanctioned throughout the society and by journalists in particular.

Now there is an important difference between these two grounds for newsworkers' reliance on bureaucratic accounts. The performative character of bureaucratic accounts is itself an adequate warrant for the journalist's acceptance of the facts in such documents: what a performative account says has to be factually correct, insofar as the society operates at all in the way newsworkers assume. However, the second basis for relying on bureaucratic accounts does not provide this strong a warrant for accepting their factual correctness. The belief that officials ought to know and ought to be recognized as knowing only allows journalists to treat bureaucratic accounts as credible but not as factually certain.

This credibility may be what draws journalists to bureaucracies for their information, but it does not assure them that what they get are necessarily the facts. Reporters often find themselves in exactly this position. Because all bureaucratic accounts do not have a performative character, what the reporter wants to know often is available only in credible accounts, not factually guaranteed accounts. Yet the newsworker is obliged to report what really happened, not what most likely happened or what could have happened. How, then, do journalists treat credible accounts as the basis for the factual stories they write?

The journalist's treatment of credible accounts hinges on the question of doubt. Reporters proceed differently depending on whether they find reasons to doubt a credible bureaucratic account. Let us now examine the nature of this doubt and reasons for it.

As stated earlier, while reporters will globally doubt nonbureaucratic accounts from the outset, they will not entertain this kind of doubt when facing bureaucratic accounts. What I mean by global doubt can best be seen in the following incident in which the justice reporter was first presented with some event through a nonbureau-cratically authorized source, i.e., a secret informant.

The Hallman Case

Justice reporter Slovekin had already submitted his news stories for the day and had returned to the newsroom from lunch. He had been working at his desk for five minutes when my field notes (Fishman 2-28-74, pp. 10–11) begin:

1:20 PM

A well-dressed young man in his thirties asked to see Slovekin at the newsroom reception desk. The secretary there sent him to Slovekin's desk. Slovekin and the man went off to talk privately.

1:30 PM

Slovekin returned to his desk, and we immediately went to the court-house. On the way there Slovekin told me to forget all about that man; forget what he looked like. He said the man had just tipped him off to "a very big case," and if anyone knew he was the source, the guy could get in a lot of trouble—he could even go to prison. Slovekin said he was going to the court clerk's office to locate some case files that the man had alerted him to.

I found out later that the tipster had been a total stranger to the reporter and that Slovekin had had no previous knowledge of what the man had told him. While Slovekin was very reluctant to tell me anything about the informant, he did tell me what the man's story was. Recently two men had been tried on charges of possession and cultivation of marijuana. Both were facing prison terms. The mari-juana was discovered after the police obtained a warrant to search their apartment for $100,000 worth of stolen paintings. No paint-ings were found in the apartment; apparently the two men had nothing to do with the theft. But they were arrested anyway for the marijuana. The police had been tipped off to find the paintings in their apartment by Jerry Hallman, a man who had turned state's evidence after his arrest for trying to sell the stolen paintings to two FBI undercover agents.

The anonymous informant told Slovekin that Hallman, who was

caught selling stolen goods, had gotten off with a year's probation, while the two men who apparently had nothing to do with the theft were facing prison sentences. Moreover, Hallman was the son of a very prominent Purissima lawyer, and at Hallman's sentencing the judge made some "very interesting" remarks indicating that the light sentence had to do with his father's status in town.

I do not know if the tipster told Slovekin to look in the court case files but that was immediately what Slovekin did after he heard the informant's account:

1:35 PM

At the court clerk's office Slovekin looked in the master index to find the case files for Hallman and the two men arrested on marijuana charges. In these case files he found the police search warrant (naming the stolen paintings being sought and the marijuana which was found). Then he started reading a long transcript of the two men's trial. Slovekin became excited. He said that the tipster was absolutely right, that there was "some pretty strong stuff in here," and that "some people" (i.e., the police and the judge on the case) were "not going to look too good" after he wrote the story.

At this point I left the reporter as he continued researching the case files.

Notice the reporter's global doubt of the informant's story. Slovekin treated his account as entirely problematic: he immediately went to check it out, to verify it as factual. No matter how plausible the story seemed, nothing in it was assumed to be true; it had no factual value per se. The informant's account was only seen as promising. It was treated as a tip or a lead to other accounts which did have a factual character, i.e., the court files. By globally doubting the informant's account, the reporter's next step in developing the story was to investigate thoroughly what he had been told. That is, the reporter set out to discover the events portrayed in a problematic account by locating them in nonproblematic, authorized sources.

Also notice what this says about the nature of tips and leads. Accounts with which reporters are presented in their routine work may be seen as either tips or potentially publishable versions of events.

What distinguishes the two types has nothing to do with something inherent in the accounts themselves. Each type of account appears the same in the sense that both are somebody's version of events, both can be sketchy versions, and both can be fraught with potential clues to further sources. What distinguishes them is the way they are subsequently treated by the reporter. A publishable version of events is an account subject to no further investigation, while a tip is an account which is globally doubted and which goes on to be redis-covered in other (potentially publishable) accounts.

To see the way reporters doubt bureaucratic accounts, let us return to the reporter's investigation of the Hallman case. As we shall see, the remainder of the investigation consisted of the reporter's reading through court case records and then verifying particular pieces of information in these files.

In an in-depth interview (Fishman 3-19-74, pp. 8–27) two days after the Hallman story was published, Slovekin explained how his investigation continued after I left him reading through the case files. He told me that that day he "really struck pay dirt in two places." The first place was the transcript of the court hearing for the two men arrested for marijuana. Here the reporter found a second transcript (within the transcript of the hearing) that the FBI made from a tape of the conversation between their agent and Hall-man as he was trying to sell the stolen paintings. Slovekin said that when he read the FBI transcript of the illegal transaction, "I knew that right then the guy was really in business for selling stolen goods. . . . That immediately told me there was a case." (Fishman interview 3-19-74, p. 9.) The second place where the reporter "struck pay dirt" was in Hallman's case files—specifically, in the probation report compiled for the judge by Hallman's probation officer. In this report the probation officer expressed reservations about the defendant's character, noting Hallman's record of two prior drug arrests, both followed by Hallman's turning state's evi-dence and receiving a light sentence.

s: For me the real break came when . . . I looked at Hallman's court file. The probation report was there, in which the probation officer severely criticized Hallman. That was good because then I could pin it on, you know, an official source. And that would soothe the nervous reaction of the editors. And that was also good stuff. . . . The probation report . . . really made me happy. That clinched the whole thing.

MF: So you didn't have to come out and say, "Hallman isn't a good probation risk." The probation officer did it for you?

S: Well who cares what I say. I'm just Joe Blow Reporter. My opinions don't carry that much weight. The probation guy deals with these people. He knows. (Fishman interview 3-19-74, p. 10.)

So far we have no evidence that the reporter doubted any of the accounts provided through the court files. This in itself is important. If Slovekin were entertaining global doubts about these accounts (as he did for his secret informant's account), then he would have tried to determine if the transcript of the FBI-Hallman conversation was authentic, or if the probation officer's assessment of Hallman's character was accurate. Instead, these accounts were treated as hard evidence that Slovekin's informant was absolutely correct. As Slovekin put it, "What more do you want?" and "The probation guy deals with these people. He knows."

These court records became the factual foundation upon which the investigation proceeded. Notice the focus of Slovekin's investigation. The critical facts were those which established Hallman as a "disreputable character." The FBI transcript was pay dirt in the sense that it established Hallman's guilt: "I knew right then that the guy was really in business selling stolen paintings." Hallman's "real guilt" was a necessary ingredient for Slovekin to continue the investigation. And the probation report "clinched the whole thing" once Slovekin saw the assessment of Hallman's character as poor. Note that the moral characters of the FBI agents and the probation officer were never doubted as anything other than reputable, fair, and professional. Slovekin took their actions toward Hallman and toward the production of Hallman's records as "motivationally transparent" (Zimmerman 1974). That is, Slovekin assumed they did just the kind of thing any professional in their position would have done, being motivated out of the routine concerns of their job. It was Hallman's character, not theirs, which was problematic. As such, anything Hallman would have to say for himself would be suspect by the very nature of the investigation.[8]

The next thing Slovekin did was to investigate specific information mentioned in the probation report—all with an eye toward establishing the disreputable character of Hallman.

S: There were a couple of other things I did, like, I really was at this point extremely suspicious of this idiot, this Hallman guy. And now, then, he had told his probation officer that he was in the National Guard. And the probation officer said he couldn't confirm or deny that. On probation reports it says what service have you been in. Well, a person can put anything there. So I called up the National Guard in Sacramento. And I got someone there to check it out for me . . . and it turned out that the guy had in fact been in the National Guard. And he was discharged honorably in 1968. He tried to give the impression he was still in it, but I didn't want to go with that story. But that's the kind of thing I was suspicious of. If I could have pinned down the fact that he was claiming to be in when he wasn't, I would have used it.
      [The second thing] I checked in the probation report is that he's now working for a guy with a known history of narcotics offenses. He's working in an auto body shop. I got the guy's name and I checked the court files on him. He is a known narcotics offender. So if I had wanted to use that I could have known in my own mind that it was true. Turned out I didn't use it. . . .
MF: Why check out the probation report? I mean, you checked out facts that it had in it. You checked out the National Guard thing. You checked out his employer. Why?
S: Well, it's always possible the probation officer can make a mistake. A good reporter always double checks.
MF: Is it possible that those court records or those transcripts that you used could make a mistake?
S: Well, they do. They frequently make mistakes in people's names. But basically I know from experience that they're basically right. And we're talkin' about a small margin of error. Basically everything they have is right. (Fishman interview 3-19-74, pp. 11–13.)

So Slovekin could question the probation report in limited ways. It could be incorrect about a few things, about details, but not fundamentally wrong. Just as in this case, I observed that for all investigations insofar as reporters are willing to doubt bureaucratic accounts, theirs is a circumscribed doubt. Even while entertaining questions about the probation report which led to further investigation, Slovekin did not doubt its essential factual character: ". . . we're talkin' about a small margin of error. Basically everything they have is right."

It is important to note why Slovekin felt the probation report could be wrong and thus deserve further investigation. The probation officer could make "mistakes" (like allowing his report to show Hallman in the National Guard), or he could "overlook" things like not checking out the character of Hallman's employer). This is, in fact, one of the two general grounds on which reporters will doubt bureaucratic accounts in circumscribed ways. They can contain occasional errors, honest mistakes, and oversights. Later we shall see how such things are detected in bureaucratic accounts and how they are handled in further newswork.

The second general ground on which journalists can and will entertain doubts about bureaucratic accounts has to do with the assumption that other (competent) perspectives on some matter may exist. Newsworkers know that any account, including a bureaucratic one, may be based on a single perspective or viewpoint and that there can be other competent accounts which differ, conflict, or simply provide other information. Thus, the existence or possible existence of other, differing bureaucratic accounts provides the newsworker with grounds for investigating beyond any one competent version.

Look at the way Slovekin proceeded to check out the probation report. He went to the National Guard to find out what they knew of Hallman's military service. Then he went to police records to see what they knew of Hallman's employer. Similarly, after Slovekin checked out possible errors in the probation report, he spent the next few days examining files in other agencies and interviewing people who all had dealt with Hallman as a disreputable character: he spoke with three Purissima police officers who were part of Hallman's stolen paintings arrest; he talked to the deputy district attorney who prosecuted the case; he interviewed Purissima's city attorney who had investigated one of Hallman's prior narcotics offenses; he asked the *Record*'s Santa Teresa reporter to look into Hallman's records at Santa Teresa municipal court; and he read Hallman's case file at the federal district court in Los Angeles. All these were competent sources that could provide accounts of Hallman from perspectives other than that of the probation officer.

Here the reporter's doubt on grounds that other perspectives exist was not specifically a doubt that the probation officer might have willfully distorted the facts. Rather, it was doubt based on the assumption that the probation officer only would see certain things about Hallman because, in the routine performance of his duty, the officer was concerned only about certain matters.

s: I'm gonna double check. Uh, if something rings a bell to me, something suspicious, even if the probation officer says it's so, I'm still suspicious. I'll double check.

MF: Is it that you would almost be treating the probation officer as an advocate, in a sense?

s: An advocate of his own view of the case. He's not supposed to be an advocate. He works for the court. He's the court's employee. (Fishman interview 3-19-74, p. 13.)

As we have seen, a single bureaucratic account of some event is usually adequate for newsworkers' purposes of reporting the facts. Usually adequate here means adequate unless there are special reasons for doubting the account in circumscribed ways. I have shown that for reporters there are at least two such special reasons. First of all, officials may commit occasional errors and oversights, and, second, there may be other competent accounts which conflict with the first bureaucratic account. Once a bureaucratic account can be so doubted, it becomes a matter for further investigation. Each of the two special reasons for doubt entail different investigative procedures. Let us now turn to these two kinds of news investigation.

5. Methods for Investigating and Formulating Stories

Irregularities and Missing Information: Filling-in

The question of seeing internal inconsistencies in bureaucratic accounts is closely tied to the matter of how reporters see anything in bureaucratic accounts. In other words, the explanation of how reporters detect irregularities is based mainly on the analysis in Chapter 3 of how journalists interpret activities as meaningful events.

Reporters rely upon various sorts of typifications of objects, actors, and actions to make sense of, and to see irregularities in, the accounts they receive. Phase structures—common sense or bureaucratic—are one very important kind of typification that the reporter uses as a resource for detecting irregularities. Of course, the reporter draws on a variety of typifications, not just familiar phase structures learned through the agencies of the beat. Examining the Hallman case again, we can see some of the ways this works.

In coming across the FBI transcript of Hallman's attempt to sell stolen paintings, it did not seem bizarre, suspicious, or curious to the reporter that an FBI agent would be wired to record a transaction with a suspect. The normalcy of FBI actions could be seen by regarding the actors involved as social types, i.e., a suspect and an FBI agent. However, the probation officer's account that Hallman was in the National Guard and gainfully employed appeared suspicious or out of character given the reporter's developing sense of Hallman as a disreputable social type: the kind of man who would deal in narcotics and stolen paintings, who would turn informer on his buddies, is the kind of man who could lie about his military service to a probation officer, and who could be doing more than merely fixing cars at his boss' auto shop. Reporters see participants in the events they investigate as social types with typical interests and motives, likely ways of acting, and so forth. They use this knowledge not only to spot inconsistencies in accounts but also as the basis for further investigation and formulation of the news story.

To explore the matter further, let us examine four cases from Wieder's field notes in which the police reporter detected inconsistencies in bureaucratic accounts. In the first case, a murder story, the police reporter discovered something strange and interesting in police field reports by noting an inappropriate delay in the reported sequence of events.

Case 1

The police report [a field investigation of the murder, which the reporter was reading] first gave the sequence of events that police went through: the time that they had gone to the hotel, exactly what they had encountered, and the persons that they talked to. And then it reconstructed the sequence of known events, starting from the previous night, and so forth. . . .

One of the facts that is included in the police report is that there is a two-hour delay between the time that the body was first discovered and the time at which the police were called, *although it is not referred to in the account as a delay*. Instead, it is referred to by telling the time at which the body was first discovered, then telling the time the police were called. . . .

The reporter is a bit troubled by this. He says: "Hell, it isn't that important anyhow." But then he does decide to put it in [his story]. . . . Later, the reporter thought that it was very, very strange, and that it was an interesting part of the story. . . .

[Back in the *Record* newsroom] the reporter has a chance to talk to some of the [other] reporters and the city editor [to whom he has submitted the murder story]. The city editor spots immediately the strange timing. . . . As the police reporter goes on his way out to lunch a copyreader stops him and notes the strangeness of that elapsed amount of time. (Wieder field notes 11-13-64, pp. 15–16.)

Note that the inferred delay could loom large as a strange and interesting detail only with reference to the duration of some typical event included within a common sense phase structure associated with people's discovery of murder: first you find the body, then you call the police, and so on. This "delay" was seen specifically with reference to the reporter's knowledge of typical durations between the phases of action: two hours between the two phases was too long; it constituted a delay; something strange was going on with the participants; something noteworthy happened. Recall that the assumption that there are typical durations between phases is one of the five general features of all phase structures. Thus, perceiving a violation of one of the general properties of phase structures is one of the fundamental bases upon which irregularities can be detected in accounts.

Now notice how the reporter handled the irregularity. He simply included it as a fact in his news story without further explanation. At the point the reporter detected the delay he had no time to stop writing the story and investigate the matter. He left it open for the time being. It is unclear whether he investigated the matter later on or simply waited to see if it would be cleared up by the police in their further investigations. Nevertheless, this demonstrates one way of handling such irregularities: leave it open, wait and see.

Actually, as Wieder noted in the description of the incident, the reporter did something more than just wait and see. He defined it as a matter to be waited upon, to be explained, and he formulated it in his story as an interesting delay. To do this he had to fill in something in the police report that was not there. We shall see that such filling-in is a very general procedure reporters use to handle irregularities in bureaucratic accounts. In many cases, as in the present incident, the procedure of filling-in is used to formulate another interesting fact of the case to be included in a news story. The typifications that allow the reporter to see the irregularity are the same typifications drawn on to fill in the missing information. In the next case, a similar instance of filling-in was used toward a somewhat different end.

Case 2

While the reporter was writing up a story from a police investigation report of a grand theft, he turned to the researcher and said: "Frequently the most interesting part of the story is what the police don't say. And you can write about what they don't say. In this case [the grand theft] there are no clues to who took the property." The reporter wrote in his story on the theft that "The police have no clues in the case," even though the police report does not say this. It just makes no reference to clues whatsoever. The researcher then asked the reporter if he routinely does this sort of thing: "Yes, I use that frequently. I think most people do. For example, in a fight, if the police don't state a reason you can say that the attack was 'without reason,' 'a senseless beating,' or 'a vicious beating,' even though the police haven't said this" (based on Wieder field notes 11-11-64, pp. 1–2).

Here the reporter's filling-in work is used not so much to remedy and reformulate something strange or irregular as to add something interesting to a news story that was left out or overlooked in the original account. Again, for the reporter to have seen something missing, he had to rely on his knowledge of the structure of typical police practices in certain kinds of cases (e.g., grand thefts). Against this background the journalist saw what was excluded in one particular account of an actual case. The reporter had to know that part of the investigation phase for grand theft phase structures is the search for clues and the reporting of them in an investigation report. He had to know that if no clues are found, no clues are reported. And he assumed this on the basis that the search for clues and the reporting of them are procedural obligations of police. In short, the filled-in information—that when no clues are reported, no clues have been found—was provided by the reporter's knowledge of "proper" police procedure.

Case 3

The third case demonstrates a similar basis for the journalist's filling-in work as well as some of the options the reporter has in dealing with missing information. The reporter was writing a story about a meeting held by the district attorney for local law enforcement chiefs. At the meeting the D. A. spoke about Purissima's election code and how it applied to an upcoming election.

[The reporter has written] in his article that the police will maintain strict surveillance of the precincts. Now, the reporter has called the Chief [of Police] to check with him to make sure this is so. He says he hopes that it is. In order to get the story in, because the Chief hasn't called him back immediately, he toned down the sentence to say that they will surveil the polls. He says he can assume that is so because that is their job. The reporter then turns the story in. (Wieder field notes 10-30-64, p. 6.)

The district attorney's original account said nothing of what the police would do, only what the law was. In making a story of it, the reporter filled in the new piece of information on the basis of normal police procedure. Here, normal procedure does not mean what the reporter knew the police to have actually done in the past; it is not some "mental average" of known police practices. Rather, as in Case 2, normal procedure means what the reporter knew to be the normatively provided-for actions of the police, what they ought to be doing. Just the knowledge that "it's their job" was enough evidence for the reporter to write that "they will surveil the polls."

Also notice that before the reporter went ahead and wrote this filled-in information as a fact of the story, he tried to talk to the police chief, i.e., he tried to do further investigation into the matter. By finding another authoritative perspective on the event (besides the D. A.'s), he could write more on the issue of "what the police will do." But, again, the reporter had to let it pass for lack of time; his own filling-in had to be good enough. In theory, at least, reporters can do extensive investigation of irregularities or missing information in accounts by turning to other perspectives on the event. What this kind of investigation entails is a matter to be taken up in the next section. But first let us consider the fourth and final case.

Case 4

This incident shows the reporter's more extensive use of phase structures as means for translating a sketchy police report into an appropriate news story. The reporter had recently written a story about a certain con game played on local residents. Soon thereafter on his round through sheriff's headquarters a detective showed the journalist a police report about an unsuccessful attempt to use the same con game on a man (referred to as Mr. Donato).

A detective comes into the reporter's office at the sheriff's headquarters with a report in his hands saying, "Did you see this about this suspicious man?" The reporter says, "No." Then the detective answers, "Maybe your article saved that joker some money." He hands the reporter the report. The reporter scans it, saying, "That is good."
. . . The police report said that Donato was approached by another Spanish-speaking man who asked him, after some preliminary conversation, where he kept his money in the bank, how much he had, and how much interest he got. What the would-be victim did next was not said in the police report. The police report merely said that fifteen minutes later

or so Donato arrived at the police station. The reporter later wrote in his story, "At this point, police reported, Donato left and called police, but they could not locate the man." Although how the conversation between Donato and the suspect was terminated was not included in the police report, *the reporter supplied the transition between the two phases* that were mentioned in the police report. The first phase, that there was a conversation. The second phase, Donato's arrival at the police station. When I asked the reporter about his use of the phrase "at this time," the reporter said that he can reasonably assume that something like this happened. . . . The reporter also pointed to the fact that the incident was reported to the police by Donato fifteen minutes later.

The next section of the reporter's story continues: "If the ruse had succeeded, police said, the bunco artist would later have 'handkerchief-switched' Donato's savings for a wad of newsprint cut to dollar bill size." Now, the police report didn't say anything about what would have happened if Donato's conversation with the suspect had continued, and the reporter also did not ask the police *this time*. Just last week, however, the reporter did a story on con artists, and now he uses the knowledge that he obtained to identify this incident *as to type*, in order to "fill in" the rest of the phases of the sequence had it continued. (Wieder field notes 11-12-64, pp. 2–3.)

In two places the reporter did filling-in on the basis of two different phase structures. First, he supplied the transition between two stages in a common sense phase structure: the con man's approach to Donato and Donato's arrival at the police station. As we saw in Case 1, here again the reporter was relying on one of the five general properties of all phase structures. In this case it is the principle that there must be continuity between phases. And the reporter supplied what that continuity according to common sense had to be. Again, it is instructive to compare this case with Case 1. Far from seeing the fifteen-minute duration between the two phases as a strange delay, the reporter saw it as further evidence that this was a certain kind of phase structure in which fifteen minutes was not only an appropriate duration but also was the same fifteen minutes taken up by the next phase of action missing in the police report (i.e., leaving the con man to go to the police).

The second place the reporter did filling-in was where he used the event phase structure of the con game to add what would have happened to Donato had the con game continued. As Wieder points out, the reporter was using a recently learned typification to identify the present incident as an instance of the same type of thing. The interactional basis of such typifications is important. The reporter first learned the con game phase structure from police who explained it to him as a certain kind of con game. A week later the reporter saw the same con game when a detective showed him a police report, pointing it out as an instance of the same kind of thing.

I have only presented the broad outlines of how reporters detect and deal with irregularities and missing information in bureaucratic accounts. Although further research needs to be done in this area, we now know that journalists detect irregularities or see missing information by drawing on their knowledge of actors as social types and activities as typical events in phase structures. At least with respect to typifications of activities, the five general properties of phase structures apparently provide rules, the violation of which constitutes irregularities in accounts.

The typifications which the reporter uses derive both from common sense and bureaucratic definitions of actors and events. We saw the police reporter employing common sense phase structures associated with the discovery of murders (Case 1) and con games (Case 4). But we also saw him relying on police categories of crime. The reporter filled in missing information in police reports by using the police conception of a certain kind of con game (Case 4). In order to see what was "missing" from an official investigation report, the reporter relied on the police category of grand theft and the bureaucratic phase structure associated with it (Case 2).

Moreover, these typifications are not necessarily stable nor are they knowledge fixed in the head of the reporter. In the Hallman case the reporter was continually developing a sense of Hallman as a social type (and, by contrast, law enforcement personnel as opposite social types) in the course of inspecting documents and interacting with officials. Similarly, the con game phase structure (Case 4) was learned as a type of structured action in the course of the reporter's work with police. Thus, to say that new typifications develop in the course of actual newswork is to say that the reporter learns them mainly through agencies on the beat.

The same typifications which enable reporters to detect irregularities provide them with the resource for handling these irregularities in further newswork. Upon encountering an irregularity in bureaucratic accounts, the general procedure is to fill in what could be or what must be going on, and this information is drawn from the same typification that led the journalist to see the irregularity in the first place.

Reporters will do at least one of two things once they have such filled-in information. First of all, they can remedy the "error" or add the "missing information" to the news story they write. In this instance, they are reformulating "new" and "interesting" facts of the case. Or, second, they can make the filled-in information the basis for further investigation by turning to other perspectives on the event which could provide different accounts. To a large extent, the choice of which to do is determined by whether the reporter believes there is enough time to find other sources, read other documents, and interview other officials.

Thus, the first of the two reasons for investigating bureaucratic accounts (that they may contain irregularities) turns out to lead to the second reason for investigation (that other differing accounts on the event may exist).

The Perspectival Nature of Events: Fact-by-Triangulation

In common sense reasoning, as well as in theorizing by philosophers of science, facts are statements. They are not the thing-in-itself but depictions of the thing-in-itself. They are not the "observables" but are hopefully accurate and true formulations of the observables. Insofar as there can be more than one way to depict what's going on, journalists (among others) face a significant problem: Which of two or more possible depictions of the facts should be sought in an investigation or should be written in a news story? To understand journalists' ways of dealing with this problem we need to examine the newsworker's conception of how more than one version of the facts can exist.

Newsworkers account for different depictions of fact and different versions of an event by a simple principle: the world is available to be known from a variety of perspectives. Different versions of what happened are explained in terms of different perspectives from which the self-same thing is seen[1] and described. In line with what Pollner (1970) calls "the presuppositions of mundane reasoning," journalists will not entertain the notion that the presence of different, even conflicting, accounts of an event indicate that what happened could be more than one actuality, that the thing-in-itself could really be more than one thing at the same time. Although they might philosophize about the issue on their days off, as a practical consideration in doing investigative work reporters will not consider that different versions of events indicate different realities.

The practical issue for newsworkers is how to treat the differing versions of events. But the critical question underlying this practical issue is: Why do different perspectives on a single event arise in the first place? What is their source? The newsworker's determination of the nature of the perspective is crucial in determining the facticity of the account, whether to use it, and how to use it as the basis for a news article.

My data show that journalists employ at least the following conceptions of the origin of different perspectives on a single event. (All of the below should be read with the preface, "according to the journalist. . .")

1. *Different perspectives may be attributable to differences in observers' "positions" from which they perceive something.* "Position" is meant here as:

   a. *A physical location:* Observers may know only partial or differing aspects of what happened because of their respective lines of sight, obstructions of view, distances from the event, interfering noises, etc.

   b. *A temporal location:* Observers may know only partial and differing aspects of what happened because of differing time frames in which they saw the event in progress. For example, one person saw it in its early phase, one person saw it in a later phase, and a third person saw it for its entire duration.

2. *Different perspectives may represent differential "competence" of observers.* "Competence" is meant here as:

   a. *An innate competence:* Some observers are blind, deaf, senile, addled, forgetful, sleepy, stupid, distracted, boastful, and inarticulate. Others are not.

   b. *An experiential competence:* Some individuals have less experience with the kind of event they saw, while others are veteran observers. Novices may get things wrong because they do not know the broader context and deeper background of the events they observe.

c. *A social structural competence*: Some observers are in social structural positions to know what's going on better than others not in those positions. That is, personal knowledge and expertise, as well as access to information, is bureaucratically organized and distributed. (This is the same sense in which I discussed competence earlier in Chapter 4.)

3. *Different perspectives may represent the different interests of observers in what they saw.* Interested observers may see what they want or hope to see, or see only the few things they have an interest in seeing. Furthermore, observers' interests may lead them to distort, change, selectively present, or outright lie about what they have seen when they give an account of it.

Although journalists may take these conceptions as adequate explanations of why they continually run into alternative and competing versions of events, their real practical value for reporters lies in their use as grounds for deciding whether to dismiss an account as useless, treat it as a factual or partially factual report, or treat it as but one side of a story of which all sides need to be told. Thus, reporters' sense of the perspectival nature of accounts is critical if they are to guide themselves through an investigation into a formulated story. It not only informs them of how to regard individual accounts but also of where to go next in seeking appropriate sources, as well as how to regard any source's account in relation to other accounts and in relation to the story as a whole.

Let us now turn to each type of perspectival account—the "incompetent," the "positional," and the "interested"—to examine the ways reporters treat them in investigating and formulating a story.

Incompetent Perspectives and Incompetent Accounts

Discrepant accounts which are seen to differ because of the differing competence of observers are handled quite simply. Less competent or incompetent sources will be ignored, discounted, or never sought out in the first place. As we have seen in Chapter 4, the competence of the news source is critical for determining the facticity of any account. Less competent sources are generally worthless to the reporter. From a journalistic point of view, the less competent account cannot be trusted to provide facts, nor is it potentially publishable as one side of the story. The competence of the news source is a prerequisite to the acceptability of the account. Even if there are other reasons one version differs from other versions of the event (e.g., the account also stems from a positional or an interested perspective), as long as that account is seen as incompetent it can be discounted altogether.

Reporters recognize competence in sources largely by recognizing the structural or official position, if any, that the source's account represents. This consideration—that sources be in an official position of knowledge—is so crucial that it seems to override other evidence which might suggest that an official is incompetent on other grounds. For example:

During his recent struggle to remain chairman of the House Banking Committee, 81-year-old Wright Patman paid a quiet visit to House Speaker Carl Albert in an effort to enlist his support. Walter Taylor, an able and respected reporter for *The Washington Star-News*, heard of the meeting and stationed himself outside the Speaker's office. When Patman emerged, Taylor asked him how he had fared. "Yes," said the old man, "Speaker Rayburn will vote for me."

Sam Rayburn was Speaker of the House for 17 years in the 1940's and 1950's. He had been dead since 1961. Taylor pressed Patman further, asking whether Albert would merely vote for him or work actively for his reelection as Banking chairman. Patman responded evasively, but again referred to Albert as "Speaker Rayburn." Patman's slips came as no great surprise to Taylor, for the chairman had for some time been regarded by reporters covering the House and by many Congressmen as senile. But there was no mention in Taylor's story the next day of the "Speaker Rayburn" episode (Hume 1975).

Nevertheless, competence for journalists is not completely a matter of one's authorized (social structural) position to know. It also includes what I have termed innate and experiential competence. Thus, reporters must have ways of assessing competence outside bureaucratic frameworks of official knowers. As we saw with Slovekin's unauthorized secret informant in the Hallman case, the reporter deemed this source competent enough to warrant further investigation of his account. Now it is true that Slovekin only used the informant's account as a lead, i.e., as a less competent account to be discarded after other more competent accounts could be located which retold the same story. Even so, if all unauthorized accounts were automatically deemed incompetent, then we could not explain their value as leads and tips. Similarly, if all unauthorized sources were automatically deemed incompetent, we could not explain why an eyewitness or the man in the street sometimes constitutes an appropriate source for news stories.

Reporters' ways of assessing competence are not clear at this point—probably because the matter is not entirely clear to journalists themselves. For example, Tuchman (1969) points out there was considerable disagreement and uncertainty among newsworkers as to whether anti–Vietnam War groups were competent sources to provide perspectives on the Vietnam War. In general, the assessment of competence by journalists, or by anyone else in the society, has an open-ended quality: someone previously seen as competent can always be reevaluated as incompetent in light of new evidence. But how is such new evidence seen and how is it made the basis of any reassessment of competence? Undoubtedly, the issue for reporters is tied up with the more general question of how any member of society assesses another member's competence to provide accounts. As yet, sociologists have only begun to answer this question.

Positional Perspectives and Positional Accounts

Consider the way one reporter used his perspectival sense of accounts to investigate and plot the progress of a forest fire:

> The reporter, with his staff artist beside him [who is] working on a map of the [forest] fire, calls various guard stations around the perimeter of the fire. He knows these people by their names. . . . He asks them what they can see from their vantage point, like, he asks, "Can you see smoke?" The staff artist tries to get the reporter to get as exact a position as possible of whatever the guards can see. (Wieder field notes 10-1-64, p. 10.)

The method in use here presupposes that the various sources (fire lookouts) and their accounts will differ because of their different positional perspectives on the event. I shall call this technique the fact-by-triangulation method of news investigation. We shall see its more general applicability later, but for now let us examine its characteristics.[2]

The method requires that reporters repeatedly employ the following two-step procedure to guide their investigative work, to locate their sources, and progressively to pinpoint the facts:

1. Who would competently know X?
2. What aspects of X would they know given their positional perspectives?

The first step of the procedure is a very general one, used in practically all investigative work. (Recall the reporter's investigation of fire damages in Chapter 2.) As we can see in the present case competent knowers are official sources, i.e., designated lookouts and not just random bystanders. This is, of course, critical to the use of the fact-by-triangulation method because reporters only assume triangulation will work if their sources' accounts have a factual character, which depends on their competence as observers.

The second step of the procedure gives the method its special perspectival character. Through it, reporters assume they will get differing accounts and that these differences are caused by the differing positions of the observers. Again, these assumptions are critical because without them the differing accounts could be attributed to the bias or incompetence of each individual observer. Moreover, if the accounts did not differ, the method would not work. Thus, the reporter tries to elicit differing accounts to determine the facts. That they differ does not detract from their facticity. Reporters are not thinking along the lines, "Which account is the correct one?" They are assuming that all are correct and that the facts provided in each can be merged into one factual news account (e.g., the map of the fire and its accompanying story). To make the fact-by-triangulation technique work, the reporter must have ways to insure that the differing aspects of events that sources provide are comparable. The journalist must appeal to some common frame of reference to bring each fact into correspondence. Both reporter and lookout must be relying on certain shared schemes of direction and distance (e.g., "I can see smoke two miles to the north."). But it is not so apparent in the present case that the reporter takes pains to insure that all observers use shared frameworks of direction and distance. Journalists probably need not do so because all competent members of this society (reporters and fire lookouts included) are expected to use culturally shared schemes of direction, distance, and time. However, as the following news dispatch from a Washington *Post* reporter in Cambodia shows, Western journalists in non-Western societies may sense acutely the problem of not being able to rely on taken-for-granted, shared schemes of time, distance, and direction from otherwise competent observers.[3]

FACTS ARE FEW: CAMBODIA—WAR OF THE PHANTOMS
by H.D.S. GREENWAY

KOMPONG SPEU, CAMBODIA—The woman was talking about an air strike. It had been on a village perhaps three villages from her own and she had seen the flames in the sky, she said, and the sound was like thunder.

How many were killed? Has she actually seen the bodies?

No, she hadn't actually seen them but she had heard people say there were many dead.

Two diplomats from the American Embassy, both fluent in Khmer, had driven down from the capital to talk to refugees about the effects of the American bombing.

They sat talking to the woman under a thatched roof in the courtyard of a small pagoda or wat, as they are called here. The saffron-robed monks, their heads shaved, sat still and tried to keep cool in the heat of noon. They were sipping hot tea from little cups. The wat was old, with deep red tiles on the roof. A dog of uncertain breed, common to all of Indochina, lay sleeping in the shade, unaware of the flies.

How far away was the air strike? Several people suggested a distance. One man scratched in the dirt with a stick drawing a map, but nobody really knew. The monks said the bombs landed close enough so that the dust kicked up by the explosions reached the wat on the wind.

It is ever so in Cambodia. "How far did you walk from your village to get here?"

"Oh, I walked a long time."

"But how long did you walk? How far?"

"I walked so far that my whole body ached and until I was so tired."

Distance, time, numbers—all the things that are important to bureaucrats in Washington—are not important to Cambodians and cannot be calculated. . . . (Los Angeles *Times*, April 29, 1973, Part I, p. 1.)

Even within their own society, however, when reporters need to compare differing accounts on some basis other than culturally shared schemes of direction, time, and distance, they must actively work to establish among their sources a common frame of reference for accounts.

Interested Perspectives and Interested Accounts

Reporters also use the fact-by-triangulation method to ascertain the facts in cases where competent knowers are likely to have interested perspectives on some event. What this actually means is that aspects of differing accounts can be triangulated into facts not only where physical and temporal locations of sources differ, but also where the social structural positions of sources differ. People are assumed to know different aspects of an event because of what part they would typically play in it, how they would typically come to know it, and for what typical purposes they would know it.

The journalist assumes that observers' social structural positions induce particular and typical interests in observers. For example, a defense attorney, simply by virtue of his or her structural position in a legal case (leaving aside the question of any personal bias), would be seen as having an interested perspective on the case. This kind of interested perspective is assumed to have *some* factual value because it is a structurally induced interest. In contrast, an interested perspective attributable to personal bias or corruption is assumed to be suspicious and of indeterminate factual character.

Reporters assume that they can use the triangulation method for interested accounts because they assume that accounts issuing from interested perspectives can have some factual value provided that the interests they represent are structurally induced. Thus, the use of the triangulation technique depends on the newsworker's knowledge of the variety of social structural locations from which an event can be viewed and the typical ways in which those locations provide for typical interests in the event.

For example, note the way one reporter said he would investigate a schoolyard gang fight.

I asked the reporter . . . if he were going to investigate rumbles how he would go about it. He said he would go to the school and talk to kids, who would probably over-blow it, and then he would talk to the principal of the school which the fighters come from and get information from him. The principal would probably down-play it. He would also talk to the police whose view he would trust, but it would not be in detail enough. (Wieder field notes 10-8-64, p. 7.)

The whole matter here is conceived structurally, not only in terms of what perspectives to seek out, but also in terms of what kinds of distortions in which kinds of accounts are expectable given the structurally induced interests and sentiments of each party.

In the earliest stages of organizing an investigation, reporters assemble a constellation of interests around a given event in such a way that they can triangulate in on the facts of the case. Precisely by conceiving of interested perspectives in social structural terms the reporter is able both to identify a set of competent and relevant interests and to trust that their differing accounts reveal differing factual aspects of the event.

In the next case studied, a police reporter was covering a civil legal matter. The journalist's active assembly of a constellation of interests around an event will not be so apparent in this case for two reasons. The first is that the reporter had already been covering the matter at earlier stages of its event career. Thus, he approached the next installment with an already formulated, historically developed constellation of interests. The second and more important reason is that, because the reporter took the matter to be a product of the civil justice system, the exact number, identity, and character of interested parties were already formulated for him by the judicial agents handling the case. That is, the civil justice system not only organized the event, it also organized the constellation of interested account-givers for the reporter. Nevertheless, this case clarifies the particular way in which reporters apply the fact-by-triangulation method to multiple accounts stemming from interested perspectives.

The county of Purissima passed an ordinance to ban roadside billboards. A billboard company took the matter to court. As soon as the judge handed down a ruling in favor of the county, the *Record*'s police reporter started to work on the story. He went first to the office of the deputy county counsel who represented the county in the law suit. The reporter asked the counsel when the order to remove billboards would go into effect, whose signs would be involved, and what legal recourse the billboard companies had. The counsel answered these questions and noted that the companies had sixty days to appeal the ruling. On his own initiative, the counsel went over the judge's decision point by point, explaining to the reporter what he considered the most newsworthy parts of the ruling.

The reporter then returned to the newsroom to call the attorney for the billboard company that had lost the case. "Hello, Mr. Gunnarson. This is Wilbur Cox from the *Record*. Do you intend to appeal this case on the billboards? I understand you have sixty days to appeal. Is that right?" The attorney said that it was correct and that they would appeal within sixty days. The rest of the telephone interview continued in a similar fashion. After stating something the county counsel had just told him, the reporter would ask, "Is that correct?" The billboard attorney then would agree or disagree (based on Wieder, field notes 10-7-64, pp. 10–11).

Even though the county counsel and the billboard attorney were seen to represent opposing interests, the reporter took as facts those aspects of each party's account which were in agreement. What the significant parts of the judge's ruling were, which and whose billboards were affected, when the signs would have to come down, and what the alternative courses of action for the sign companies were all became the facts. In general, reporters take the aspects of the event which all parties agree upon as the facts. And, as we shall see, reporters take the aspects of the event which parties differ on as the different sides of the issue.

Not to be overlooked in the billboard case is the way that the reporter actively worked to make the fact-by-triangulation method apply. He went to one party, the county counsel, to work out just what the relevant facts were according to him. Then he went to the other party, the attorney for the billboard company, and confronted him with this information, asking "Is that right? Is that correct?" The reporter did not ask each party what was happening and then try to merge their accounts. He actively set up the correspondence between accounts by treating the information learned in one interview as the basis for questions in the next. By arranging the correspondence in this way, one party's definition of the event implicitly takes priority. The grounds upon which the other parties may agree and may differ are established once the first party is interviewed.

It is no coincidence that in the billboard case the reporter chose to go first to a governmental agency, the county counsel's office. The reporter assumed—and was not disappointed in his speculation—that the counsel's formulation of the event would not be arbitrary or interested in a way that would make this first account hopelessly incomparable with the next account by the billboard attorney. The reporter was counting on the fact that the counsel's account would be in the same legal-bureaucratic terms that had been used to formulate the case throughout its event career. In fact, to help insure this, in his phone conversation with the counsel the reporter made clear his orientation toward the legal-bureaucratic facts of the case by expressing an interest in seeing the judge's written opinion.

In the next case the same reporter was setting up an investigation for a story about the local impact of recent court rulings on the legal rights of suspects in criminal cases. This investigation is more revealing of the active ways in which the journalist assembles a constellation of interests around an issue. The events involved were being covered for the first time by the reporter. Moreover, there was no agency within the reporter's beat territory which had claimed the issue as part of its bureaucratic work. Thus, no authoritative source had defined the interested parties.

[After reading today's edition of the *Record* the reporter] clips one UPI story which is headed "Police Hampered by Court Rulings." . . . Then he writes a note to the city editor on a possible story that he might do on these court rulings from the point of view of the police and the point of view of civil rights. In the note he phrases it in terms of the questions that could be posed. "What the police think about the way in which these things have hampered them and what they still have at their disposal," and "What the point of view of the opposition of the police think about the rulings." Then he delivers this note to the city editor. . . .

[Later, after the reporter returns to the newsroom from lunch] there is a note in his mailbox. . . . Written on the note that the reporter had given the city editor earlier is typed: "Sounds good. Overcome your convictions and ideas. I'm sure that you can do that." . . . The city editor comes over and talks to the reporter. He said, "Right-thinking people like us, of course, are all for civil rights, but the point of view of the poor cop has to be brought out. You know. They have their troubles." . . .

[Forty-five minutes later] the reporter begins to plot out the story on police vs. citizen's rights. He first begins to list those persons who would hold authoritative opinions on the matter to be covered. He asks me if I know of a sociologist who would be such an authority. I tell him about Oliver Lackland, the criminologist, now at Boulder Beach University. I also suggest there may be some political scientists at Boulder Beach University and at the Laguna Perdida Institute who might hold strong opinions on the matter. I also suggested to him the local ACLU. He listed all of these. On the list that he had already developed he had Judge Janowski, the Sheriff, the District Attorney, and the Police Chief. For some reason he lists Leopold and Loeb and Clarence Darrow. He tells me that he has just read a book about this case. Perhaps he is going to draw some quotes about this case. I ask him who he is going to talk to on the prosecution side of the issue, and he tells me besides the police, sheriffs, and District Attorney, he will talk to Judge Prince. "He is pretty much prosecution minded." I suppose that he is listing Judge Janowski for the opposite reason.

[Later, to set up future interviews with the prosecution side of the story] he calls the Police Chief and tells him of the story that he wants to write. He wants to talk to the Chief about the big obstacles that these [court] decisions have produced for the police, and the weapons that they still have left in law enforcement. . . . Then he calls the D. A. and asks for his help. He asks that maybe someone could help him prepare a list of these court decisions that have made obstacles and a list of the tools that they still have. Then he calls the Sheriff and he tells him the same thing. (Wieder field notes 10-28-64, pp. 10–14.)

Throughout this case the reporter sets up his story-to-be-written in the same process that he defined its topic and organized his investigation. From the outset the story-to-be-written was conceived in terms of opposing viewpoints and the questions he would ask people holding those viewpoints. In other words, the story was being defined in terms of how it would be investigated. Moreover, at the point at which the story was conceived, the reporter was looking for a balance of viewpoints. The sides of the issue would be presented and distributed equally throughout the story-to-be-written. In approving the story idea, the city editor also stressed the necessity of this balance.

Thus, there was a concern for locating and presenting a variety of perspectives from which the issue could be seen—perspectives which offered differing accounts which would balance one another in the story to be formulated. Not just any opposing perspectives would do. The reporter was interested only in perspectives based on the various structural positions from which the matter could be seen. Here, again, the interested parties had to be competent knowers, and this meant authoritative sources.

As the reporter continued to work on the story, he began drawing up a list of interested parties in terms of what he had formulated as the "pro" and "con" sides of the issue. In drawing up this list the reporter assembled a constellation of interests around the issue. He actively organized the phenomenon to be discovered (i.e., what the sides of the issue were) at the same time he set up his investigation of it. The nature of this assembly work is worth examining.

In this particular case we can see that the reporter's assembly of the constellation of interests to a large extent had an improvisational and idiosyncratic character. A book that the reporter happened to be reading could supply a viewpoint, and a sociologist who happened to be standing next to the reporter could recommend other academic viewpoints. In work on the same story the next day (not cited above), the reporter asked another journalist in the newsroom if he could suggest some people he knew at Laguna Perdida Institute who might be sources for the story.

Thus, in searching for sources reporters not only ask themselves "Who would know X?" but they also can embed the question within itself to extend their local resources of knowledge: Who knows somebody who knows X? Who knows somebody who knows somebody who knows X? and so on. Reporters make use of whatever immediate resources happen to be available, starting from their own particular knowledge of local social structure, to locate possible viewpoints on an event.

Bernstein and Woodward (1974: 208–210) provide another interesting example of how reporters use their knowledge of local social structure to draw up a list of potential sources for a story. At one point in their investigation of the Watergate scandal, Woodward obtained a list of the grand jurors who had been hearing evidence against Nixon's advisors. The problem was who on the list would be willing to talk to a reporter. (Grand jurors are sworn to secrecy.) Knowing none of the jurors personally, but having face sheet information on each one from court files, the reporters decided on whom to approach by viewing each juror as a local social type.

The editors and Bernstein and Woodward eliminated nearly half the members of the grand jury as too risky. Low grade civil servants—especially older ones, for instance—were accustomed to doing things by the bureaucratic book, checking with their superiors, rarely relying on their own judgment. Military officers the same. They were looking for the few least likely to inform the prosecutors of a visit. The candidate would have to be bright enough to suspect that the grand-jury system had broken down in the Watergate case and be in command of the nuances of the evidence. Ideally, the juror would be capable of outrage at the White House or the prosecutors or both; a person who was accustomed to bending rules, the type of person who valued practicality more than procedure. The exercise continued with Bernstein, Woodward and their bosses trying to psyche out strangers on the basis of name, address, age, occupation, ethnic background, religion, income level. The final choices were left to the reporters (pp. 209–210).

Any reporter's choice of interested sources, however, is not completely open-ended. All have to be competent interested sources (in a social structural position of knowledge and interest). Moreover, the journalist's freedom to construct constellations of interest around an event is considerably restricted when the event is already happening within some governmental agency in the reporter's beat territory. Issues which have found their way into the courts or legislative bodies are events with readymade, authoritatively defined constellations of interest.

In the police versus civil rights case under discussion, there is another important place in which the reporter actively organized the phenomenon to be reported as he was setting it up for investigation. After compiling the list of interested parties, he proceeded to telephone three of them—all on the "prosecution side" of the issue—to establish future interviews. In briefing them about what he was doing and what he wanted to know from them, the reporter was prompting his sources to express just those structurally induced interests in the matter that he conceived they already held. Even though the reporter assumed that their interests were induced by their structural positions, he nevertheless did some inducing of his own to guide them into expressing just those interests. Thus, the reporter helped organize the very structurally induced interests he wanted to report.

Fact-by-Triangulation as a Framework for News Investigation and Story Formulation

We have seen that insofar as reporters deal at all with multiple accounts of an event, they use a fact-by-triangulation method as a means of merging several accounts from different perspectives into one news story. Two prerequisites exist for the use of this method. First of all, all accounts must issue from competent perspectives or competent sources. Thus, accounts which differ from one another must differ on some basis other than the differing competence of the sources, i.e., they must differ because of the positional perspectives or the interested perspectives of the sources.

Second, if the triangulation method is applied to interested accounts, then the interests these accounts represent must be structurally induced (and not matters of personal bias). In other words, the reporter must conceive of the variety of interests from which any event can be viewed in terms of the variety of social structural positions of interest from which it can be viewed. These two prerequisites justify for the reporter that each differing account has at least a partial factual character, thus allowing the accounts to be merged in a way that promises a more complete picture of the event.

The fact-by-triangulation method also provides reporters with procedures for conducting their investigations and for formulating their news stories. Reporters guide themselves through an investigation by repeatedly asking themselves (or others around them) two things: (1) Who would know X? (Or, who would be in a physical location or social structural position to know X?), and (2) What aspects of X would they know, given their positional or interested perspective? Both procedures lead the reporter to four other procedures which are part of the organization and formulation of the news story.

The questions "Who knows X?" and "What do they know of X?" invite the reporter to (1) assemble a constellation of positional or interested perspectives around the event; (2) poll (interview or read the documents of) each source for their account; (3) select aspects of each account which can be compared; and (4) merge or balance the selected aspects of the accounts into a single news story. Through all these procedures the fact-by-triangulation method enables reporters to relate several differing accounts to one another in such a way that both the facts of the case and the sides of the issue emerge. That is, the news story emerges.

Because these are abstract procedures which must be applied in concrete situations, the reporter must do several other things to make the fact-by-triangulation method work in any actual investigation.

First of all, to identify a set of interested perspectives, reporters must consult their own particular knowledge of the local social structure to determine who is in a position which would induce some typical interest in the event. Reporters use this knowledge not only to locate news sources directly but also to locate persons who would (by means of their knowledge of local social structure) know of other news sources for the story. Reporters rely on immediately available resources (e.g., their own knowledge of social structure) to locate authoritative and interested perspectives. But they can extend these resources by relying on others—a friend, a colleague, a news source—to tell them who would hold an interested perspective on the event.

Second, to make the fact-by-triangulation method work, reporters need some common framework in terms of which all of the differing accounts can be compared and merged. When dealing with positional perspectives, reporters can rely on the fact that all news sources—insofar as they are competent members of the same society—will present their accounts in terms of culturally standard frameworks of time, direction, and distance. Thus, reporters have to do little or no work to insure that accounts will be in the same terms.

When dealing with interested perspectives, however, reporters do things to make differing accounts comparable. This work occurs at two points in the investigation. When they first set up interviews, reporters inform sources of the kinds of things they want the sources to talk about. Journalists orient their sources toward a certain way of looking at an event: as a legal-bureaucratic entity, as a moral issue, as a part of a historical trend, and so forth. Thus, they define for their sources the terms of an acceptable account, the terms in which all the various accounts will be framed, and the terms in which the event eventually will be described in the news story.

After initially orienting news sources, journalists actively structure the interview so that the source's talk comes out, again, in terms of a common framework. For example, in the billboard case the reporter began by cueing his first source (the deputy county counsel) to a legal-bureaucratic framework. Then, in the actual interview he centered all requests for information around a legal document, the judge's ruling. Finally, the reporter structured the second party's (the billboard attorney's) talk in the same legal-bureaucratic terms of the county counsel's account. He did this by asking the billboard attorney questions based on answers the counsel had already given. The reporter's method for structuring each account constitutes a "chaining principle": each previous account of the event is made the basis for questions answered in a next account. The judge's account was the basis for questions to the county counsel, and the counsel's answers were the basis for questions to the billboard attorney. In this way accounts are chained together in such a way that they are all comparable.

Third, and finally, for the fact-by-triangulation method to work when journalists are dealing with interested perspectives, reporters must get sources to express only what they see as the source's particular structurally induced interest in the matter. For example, in the police versus civil rights story, the reporter wanted to interview the police chief only to get his viewpoint as a police chief, and not as a father, a Jew, or a dog owner. Reporters accomplish this in the same process of orienting interviewees to the kinds of things they want them to talk about. In other words, when journalists set up and structure their news sources' talk to fit into a common framework for all accounts, they also set up and structure their news sources' talk to express only the structural interests for which the accounts are solicited in the first place.

For certain events in which interested accounts differ, reporters will not do all this work. If reporters see that an agency in the beat territory has already claimed a controversy (i.e., agency officials are investigating an event for which multiple accounts exist), then reporters will not take it upon themselves to assemble a constellation of interests around the event or establish a common framework with which accounts are brought into correspondence. This work is already done for them by officials. Agency-conducted controversies—

such as court proceedings, administrative hearings, coroners' inquests, and legislative debates—conveniently organize for reporters the sides of the issue and the terms of the controversy. Journalists may still use the fact-by-triangulation method in these cases, but they need not (or do not) work so hard to apply the method.

We saw in Chapter 4 that one way in which reporters will come to doubt a single bureaucratic account of some event is if other competent accounts are seen to exist. We have seen in the present chapter that "other competent accounts" generally means other bureaucratic accounts. Thus, it is mainly when officials and authorities conflict over an event, when there is dissension within and between agencies, that reporters see an event as a controversy and use the fact-by-triangulation method to formulate a balanced news story.

However, when officials and authorities conflict over some event, it is also likely that this conflict already occurs within, or will soon be brought within, the control of an agency on some reporter's beat (e.g., the justice reporter's courts, the city hall reporter's city council debates, etc.). The likelihood that something will be seen as a controversy is very great once the matter comes under the scope of some agency within the beat. Once it does, the sides of the issue and the relevant terms of debate are already bureaucratically defined for the reporter.

6. The Practice and Politics of Newswork

News, Ideology, and Legitimation

In this study we have seen that reporters confront a bureaucratically constructed universe which defines the following things for them:

1. Their movements through a beat territory.
2. Their exposure to news sources.
3. The meaning and relevance of what they are exposed to (i.e., their sense of something as an event and their sense of its importance).
4. What occurrences are not worth seeing (i.e., nonevents).
5. The permissible times at which events may be reported (i.e., news pegs).
6. What constitutes a factual account and, thus, what constitutes the facts of the case.
7. What constitutes a suspicious account and, thus, what constitutes a matter to be investigated.
8. What constitutes errors and oversights and, then, what constitutes their correction in news stories.
9. What constitutes a controversial matter and, then, what constitutes the sides and terms of the controversy.

This makes news ideological. As in Chapter 2, by ideological accounts I mean accounts which are produced through "procedures people use as a means not to know" (Smith 1972: 3). Newswork includes such procedures.

In the discussion of nonevents in Chapter 3, some of these procedures were examined. By adopting the schemes of interpretation and schemes of relevance employed within agencies of their beats, reporters systematically cannot and will not see as news things which might seriously challenge an agency's idealizations of what is going on and what should be happening.

Recall the case of the invisible crank at the board of supervisors meeting who proposed that the sheriff's department deserved no funding. With reference to the idealization of how budgets get processed, she was seen as disrupting the normal progression of the budget through its bureaucratic career. As a result, the supervisors made several attempts to cut off her speech and get rid of her. The supervisors worked to repair the situation, to restore it to a right state of affairs where only procedurally appropriate courses of bureaucratic action could be considered.

Significantly, the journalists at this meeting essentially acted no differently than the supervisors: they too were involved in repair work. The reporters used similar idealizations of the budget process to see that this was a sidetracking of the real issue, that it deserved no consideration other than how to eliminate the crank and repair the meeting. Not reporting the matter was a way of discouraging this and other incidents like it in the future.

Reporters clean up and repair flawed bureaucratic proceedings in their news stories. Their model of cleanliness, orderliness, and normalcy is a bureaucratic one. Making a coherent news story out of bureaucratic proceedings in this way renders matters which violate or challenge bureaucratic idealizations invisible in newspapers. Happenings outside the proper bureaucratic treatment of the case, by definition, tend to be ignored in bureaucratic settings and in news stories.

Repair work is designed to normalize activities in bureaucratic settings. Reporters do not show this repair work and the part they play in doing it because it is part of their own account-constructing work. The news story does not disclose the sense in which it is a repaired version of what happened. What newspaper readers see is normalized bureaucratic work, nothing more nor less than the orderly bureaucratic universe as it is meant to be, and as it is continually trying to be.

Repair work is not the only way in which journalists lead the public to assume that governmental agencies function "as they should." We saw in Chapter 5 that when reporters lack time to check out all the details of a story, they often fill in missing information on the basis of their knowledge of proper bureaucratic procedure. For example, when a police reporter was writing a story about an upcoming election in Purissima, he wanted to say something about police surveillance of the voting. Without time to reach the police chief, he went ahead and wrote that the police would monitor the polls. Although no one told him this, he felt safe in assuming it because it is their job to monitor the polls.

When in doubt (and when there is insufficient time to check out their doubt) newsworkers assume that a bureaucracy functions normally, i.e., according to its own idealization of its work. The assumption of proper functioning may make life easier for journalists, but it also leads them to write idealizations into their news stories as if they were facts. A normative phrase such as "the police will monitor the polls" looks to a newspaper reader like it describes police work. Thus, the news story transforms normative idealizations into descriptive statements, giving readers the impression that government functions normally.

The journalistic standards of facticity discussed in Chapter 4 have a similar effect. Bureaucratic versions of what is happening often become the only reality newspaper readers see. In basing news on agency accounts, journalists pass on to the public bureaucratic views of the world as plain fact.

The documents and oral statements found within an agency— and generated with the intent of presenting an official version of its activities—effectively idealize actual happenings and real persons subject to the agency. For the most part, these idealized accounts are produced for internal consumption, for the agency's own purposes: to code people and events as specific, procedurally defined cases which fit one of the agency's programs; to show agency workers where the case has been and where it goes next; and to demonstrate that the agency's administrative work is according to the rules and that it is discharging its responsibilities.

Of necessity, then, such accounts are idealizations because they are intended to be administratively useful, not objectively descriptive.[1] What flesh and blood persons say and do becomes an object-to-be-administered. The object can be dealt with appropriately only if reconstructed in terms of some standard vocabulary of action. If bureaucratic accounts are descriptive of anything, they indicate only an agency's official interest in (and rationale for) administering something. They tell us little if anything about that something on its own terms, as it was experienced when it happened, as anyone might know it.

Consider, for example, case histories of inmates, patients, and delinquents generated in custodial institutions. From an agency's standpoint, the case history formally records institutionally relevant facts of a person's biography which are necessary to process the person under its charge appropriately. But, as Goffman (1961: 155–158) has pointed out, case histories do not represent "fair samplings" of a person's behavior; they contain selected incidents which document some problem which the agency is empowered to deal with. Episodes of the individual's past and present life are only included inasmuch as they can be related to the problem; incidents which do not document any trouble are ignored because they are organizationally irrelevant.

Similarly, Dorothy Smith (1973: 18–19), drawing on Cicourel (1968), describes the way in which case histories restructure actual happenings so that particular occurrences are stripped of their context and then reassembled as pieces of information which show the individual as a case deserving treatment.

> [Case records] are typically structured so that all major items of information appear as predicates of the individual subject of the report. Here is an example from Cicourel's *The Social Organization of Juvenile Justice*:
>
> > Talked to Mr. J at Jr. Hi. re Audrey—he says Audrey jumped into the fight to pull white girl off Jane Johnson—(negro) who was beating up the girl's younger sister. Audrey hit the older Penn girl a couple of times and then Candy Noland took over and Audrey withdrew. Audrey was suspended the rest of the day. A couple of minor incidents since—yesterday she and some other girls jumped on a laundry truck at school and Audrey didn't obey bus driver on bus. However, Mr. J reports that Audrey's attitude was good—admitted everything and promised she wouldn't any more.
> >
> > Talked to Audrey at school—lectured her re any fighting or disobedience. Told her if she hadn't done so well up to now she would be in serious trouble. Audrey promised not to get involved in anything and "to walk away" if trouble started around her. (Cicourel, 1968: 163)
>
> As Cicourel points out, "The P.O.'s remarks . . . constitute the 'facts' of the case." These facts have been abstracted from the events as they actually happened. Clearly the original events involved a number of people, some of whom are mentioned by name, but in this report they are organized in relation to Audrey. Thus:

> Audrey jumped into the fight . . .
> Audrey hit the oldest Penn girl . . .
> Audrey withdrew . . .
> Audrey was suspended . . .
> (Audrey) and some other girls jumped . . .
> Audrey didn't obey the bus driver . . .
> Audrey's attitude was good . . .
> Audrey promised . . .

The account resulting reorganizes the original events so that they will compose into a background of which Audrey is figure. What happens and what happened become assigned to her as her trouble. It doesn't make any difference who started it, "if you hit her back you're in trouble too" (Cicourel 1968: 144). It is her record that is being thus compiled. That is a focus which was not the focus of the original events, as they were actually coming about. It is a product of the structuring procedures involved in making a report on them in the context of probation work.

The case history is organizationally useful: it presents the agency's rationale for treating the case as it has in the past and will in the future. Case records construct (or reconstruct) the individual as a problem child, a hardened criminal, or a mental case deserving treatment; they legitimate the agency's custodial relationship with the person. Case records do not reflect reality; they attempt to make reality.

Every time journalists treat bureaucratic accounts (such as case histories) as plain fact, they help an agency make the reality it wants to make and needs to make in order to legitimate itself. Thus, not only does routine news provide ideological accounts of real people and real happenings, it ends up legitimating institutions of social control by disseminating to the public institutional rationales as facts of the world. In general, by maintaining agency idealizations, the press disregards troublesome perceptions of happenings which question the validity of a bureaucratic perspective.

It is not so much that the media convinces news consumers that all is well with the present social and political order. Rather, news consumers are led to see the world outside their firsthand experience through the eyes of the existing authority structure. Alternative ways of knowing the world are simply not made available. Ultimately, routine news places bounds on political consciousness.[2]

We have seen, then, that journalists' methods for detecting events and determining facticity are integrally tied to bureaucratic idealizations of the world. Such methods lead the journalist to present an ideological view of the existing social and political order because newswork is predicated on the assumption that bureaucracies function properly. This is not to say that the press presents bureaucracies in a perfect light. Indeed, journalists will doubt official accounts, and they will question the propriety of agency operations.

However, as we saw in Chapter 4, these doubts are circumscribed. Journalists see some agencies as more credible than others, and they know bureaucratic accounts can reflect errors and oversight, corruption and malfeasance, incompetence and inexperience. Thus, newsworkers will be critical of particular agencies or specific officials. But the governmental-bureaucratic structure cannot be doubted as a whole without radically upsetting the routines of newswork. Routine news leaves the existing political order intact, at the same time that it enumerates the flaws.

The Watergate scandals are an interesting case here because of the widescale doubts they engendered among journalists. In my view, Watergate revelations almost brought newsworkers to the point of globally doubting governmental operations: almost, but not quite. Despite the massive scale of corruption, bribery, and other illegal activities, and despite evidence that previous administrations had engaged in similar activities, the issue was defined continuously around Richard Nixon and his top advisors. The press never seemed to drop the assumption that the problem was one of bad men in a good system. Thus, when Nixon was deposed, journalists proclaimed his downfall as proof that the system still works, despite the fact that the system (i.e., the Constitution) called for impeachment and trial, not resignation and pardon.

The origin of Watergate coverage further illustrates how strongly journalists depend on a bureaucratically defined newsworld. Long before the break-in and bugging of the Democratic National Committee at the Watergate building, a number of Washington journalists privately had been suspicious of Nixon administration dealings. But they could not print their suspicions. At best, a few political commentators would raise occasional questions in columns labeled as opinion.

Nixon's illegal activities eventually were reported as hard news, but not until the police (not journalists) had discovered something. (Thus, Watergate coverage originated from a police beat, not from the White House press corps.) Once under the jurisdiction of the criminal justice system, the press could report White House malfeasance as hard fact on the front page. When there was no bureaucratic forum for dealing with the issue, there was no issue. But when a variety of official agencies took over the investigation of Watergate, Nixon was fighting a losing battle in trying to contain press coverage.

We have seen that the ideological character of news and its legitimating function need not be the result of conspiracies inspired by elites to control news. Ideological hegemony in the news media can occur without the direct intervention of publishers or editors, without the existence of informal news policies into which reporters are socialized, and without secret programs in news organizations to recruit reporters sharing a particular point of view. The ideological character of news follows from journalists' routine reliance on raw materials which are already ideological.

This reliance on ideological material does not just happen. Journalists have not simply chosen bad routines which could be replaced by good ones. To understand what brings about the newsworker's reliance on bureaucratic raw materials, let us take a closer look at the structural conditions of news production.

The Sources of News Ideology

A major theme of this study has been that news is a practical organizational accomplishment and that newsworkers heavily rely on the bureaucratic definition of the phenomena they report. These observations are interrelated: the practicalities of news production tie news organizations to governmental agencies and corporate bureaucracies.

This final section offers speculation on the broad social forces which underlie the marriage of newsworker to bureaucrat and draws out the political implications of such an analysis. I discuss this by reference to three dynamics in the American news production system: the bureaucratic logic, the normative logic, and the economic logic of news reporting.

The Bureaucratic Logic of News Reporting

I began this study by examining the routine work of reporters to discover how news gets constructed out of an amorphous world of happenings. I have found that the work process of news personnel comprises only a part, albeit a critical part, of this construction process. The raw materials upon which news stories are built are themselves the result of an intricate and complex reporting apparatus within systems of criminal justice, insurance companies, welfare agencies, law firms, mortuaries, high schools, and psychiatric clinics. It is useful, then, to think of news as the outcome of two systems which produce accounts: a system of journalistic accounts and, underlying this, a system of bureaucratic accounts. How can we characterize the relationship between these two systems in the overall news production process?

The entire news production process occurs in several successive "levels," stretching from the earliest formulated account of something on up to the reporter's written news story. For example, the accounting process which underlies any one crime story can be traced through successive levels of accounts. Only the top level consists of the police reporter's work of detecting, interpreting, investigating, and formulating the story.[3] Behind the news story, inside the agencies through which the reporter first sees the story, are the bureaucratically produced accounts upon which the news will be based.

Within any single agency, the account production process occurs (and is displayed in case files) in successive stages or levels corresponding to the phases of the case in its agency career. Layer upon layer of accounts are built up for the case. Each layer is partially based on accounts from previous layers (i.e., the records of the case produced in previous bureaucratic stages) and is partially based on recently completed accounting work (e.g., new interviews with the "client.")

Moreover, the entire process often extends beyond a single agency. Any one agency adopts in whole, in part, or in a summarized version the previous agency's multilayered accounts. These become the foundation for a new account-building process for the case. For example, on the basis of police files (investigation reports, search warrants, arrest warrants, arrest reports, etc.), the courts begin to build their own layers of accounts generated from preliminary hearings, arraignments, plea bargains, and so forth. Thus, the bureaucratic account production process can be extremely complex, involving several different but interlinked agencies, each of which, for their own purposes, code and recode the case, adding new layers of accounts to the already accumulated case file.

Up to this point I have been describing newswork as just another level in the news production process. This is not quite true, because the journalistic level of account production has priority over all other levels. Ultimately, it is the journalist's work which defines and determines the chains of accounts which lead up to the published news story. Reporters follow rounds which expose them only to bureaucratically produced accounts, and they apply agency schemes of interpretation and relevance to these accounts. By doing so, the reporter makes the successive levels of bureaucratic account production the foundation for a news story. A journalist can change the sources upon which a story is based (i.e., shift from one underlying account production system to another) simply by shifting the emphasis of what the story will be about.

The newsworker can also produce accounts not based upon the prior accounts of bureaucrats. For example, the police reporter could detect, investigate, and formulate crime news without relying on the record-keeping apparatus of the police. In fact, we have seen a few instances in which reporters did do most of the account-constructing work on their own. In the story about the police versus civil rights in Chapter 5, the reporter set up a feature article on a recognized controversial issue which had not already been claimed by a beat agency. But this is not the way news is routinely generated. The police versus civil rights story was not routine news because, compared with most stories the reporter produced, it required special attention and a large amount of the reporter's time. Newsworkers distinguish these kinds of stories from routine articles by referring to them variously as projects, think pieces, or enterprise stories. In the police versus civil rights case it took the reporter days to assemble a list of sources, contact interviewees, prepare for and do the interviews, and compose the written news story. What usually takes minutes for most news takes hours or days for these kinds of stories. Reporters on the *Record* produced at most one think piece a week, compared with producing from two to six routine news stories every day.

These journalists were able to write two to six articles every day precisely because what they did was largely based on preconstituted bureaucratic accounts. As a practical matter, reporters rely on bureaucrats to do much of their account-producing work for them. It is not so much that reporters choose to base their news on already existing bureaucratic accounts. Reporters do not experience this as a decision-making matter. They experience it as a practical matter: as a matter of getting their job done and as a matter of displaying their competence to do the job.

As I pointed out in Chapter 2, under the constraints of daily story quotas and deadlines the newsworker needs "fountains of information" that dependably produce reliable quantities of raw materials every day. Bureaucracies are so organized that their account-producing systems meet these constraints in ways that other kinds of news sources cannot or do not. In other words, there appear to be no other modes of account production in this society that can provide daily newspapers with the scope, variety, dependability, and quantity of information that bureaucracies can deliver—and deliver in a scheduled, predictable way. Newspapers need bureaucracies because the journalistic system of account production is itself bureaucratically organized. The news organization needs reliable, predictable, scheduled quantities of raw materials because it is set up to process these in reliable, predictable, scheduled ways in order to turn out a standard product (the newspaper) at the same time every day. Only another bureaucratically organized system of account production could meet these needs by virtue of its self-regulated, reliable, predictable, scheduled activities.

This can be termed the principle of bureaucratic affinity: only other bureaucracies can satisfy the input needs[4] of a news bureaucracy. Whether one is turning lumber into toothpicks, people into clients, or court files into news stories, the flow of raw materials must be controlled or at least made predictable. News is made by routinizing the unexpected (Tuchman 1973). Thus, every newsworker acknowledges as a fact of life that news is slow on weekends because bureaucracies are shut down. More importantly, they can count on it. Thus, management gears down the news operation accordingly.[5]

Taken to its extreme the bureaucratic logic of news reporting would lead a news organization to bring the flow of the raw materials for news stories thoroughly under its control.[6] Curiously, this would mean eliminating such inputs altogether. All shortages and unpredictable variations in the flow of raw news could ultimately be avoided if the materials upon which news stories were based could be internally generated by the news organization. Thus, the internal pace of producing a set of news stories would no longer have to speed up, slow down, or halt because of the availability of externally generated raw materials for news.

In effect, this means newsworkers would create stories based on what they already knew about something, plus a little imagination. To a limited extent, this already goes on. Every newsroom has as part of its folklore the story about the reporter who missed the mayor's speech or the groundbreaking but wrote it up anyway based on a press release and a good guess. Interestingly, such stories often contain a punch line: the mayor gave a different speech or the groundbreaking was rained out.

That newsworkers attach a moral to such stories indicates that these practices are frowned upon. Good news practices entail going out in the world to get stories. Anything else is seen as a matter of crass expediency or downright cheating.[7] There is, thus, a normative element in newswork which, at least up until the present, has placed limits on the extreme tendencies of the bureaucratic logic of news reporting.

The Normative Logic of News Reporting

As discussed in Chapter 4, reporters are held accountable to write about real happenings using factual information. We saw that the newsworker's criteria for hard facts lead reporters to bureaucrats and officials. Newsworkers are predisposed to treat bureaucratic accounts as factual because news personnel participate in upholding a normative order of authorized knowers in the society. Reporters operate with the attitude that officials ought to know what it is their job to know, and they sanction officials for knowing or not knowing what they should. In particular, a newsworker will recognize an official's claim to knowledge not merely as a claim, but as a credible, competent piece of knowledge.

This amounts to a moral division of labor: officials have and give the facts; reporters merely get them. Reporters are not entitled to know (in the sense of hard fact) what competent sources will not or do not tell them.

In several ways this is a very convenient state of affairs. From the point of view of the individual reporter, the moral division of labor provides a way to deal with two potential problems. First, as in any work place, the reporter is potentially accountable that she or he is doing the job and doing it competently. Historically, with the advent of the beat system, the competent performance of the reporter's job has been tied to the detection, interpretation, investigation, and formulation of news events through bureaucracies. If asked to account for their whereabouts ("Where did you go and what did you do?"), they can display competence with reference to the agencies on the round of their beat ("I went to the police department and looked through arrest records").

Second, as Tuchman (1972) has pointed out, newsworkers constantly operate under the threat of criticism of bias and, ultimately, of libel suits. Insofar as newsworkers can assume that their critics uphold the same normative order of authorized knowers that they uphold, then reporters (as well as editors and publishers) have a ready-made defense for whatever is printed: "The probation officer (the President, the city administrator, the fire inspector) said so and he ought to know; if it turns out he's wrong, that's his mistake, not mine."

The normative logic of news reporting may limit the extreme possibilities inherent in a bureaucratic logic of news reporting, but in no way does it contradict the direction of a bureaucratic logic. Both systems of logic lead newsworkers straight to the files, meetings, and officials in agencies which provide safe, predictable inputs of raw news.

The Economic Logic of News Reporting

The organizational constraints on newsworkers which constitute a bureaucratic logic of news reporting can be traced to economic considerations in the management of news organizations. In other words, an economic logic of news reporting underlies the bureaucratic logic. Deadlines, story quotas, and the need for conveniently locatable, expectable, and dependable quantities of raw news all have their rationale in the capitalist economy of news enterprises. What must be examined first is the economic basis of each of these constraints; then we will be in a position to consider the overall economic logic of news reporting.

DEADLINES

The economic motive for news deadlines is clear. If a newspaper is to maintain a sizable readership, it must periodically deliver its product at predictable times and places. Moreover, news organizations aim their deliveries at specific time slots to capitalize on prime reading periods: morning newspapers must be on the streets in time for breakfast readers and commuters on their way to work; evening papers aim for a predinnertime audience, including commuters on their way home.

As Tuchman (1972: 663) points out, profits suffer when deadlines are missed not only because a loyal readership depends on reliable deliveries, but also because any disruption of the distribution system is in itself costly.

Trucks carrying the newspaper to outlying regions will leave late; their drivers will merit overtime pay. If one edition is late, the scheduling of the following editions will be affected; printers may claim overtime. Moreover, if the late morning editions do not arrive at newsstands on schedule, consumers may buy the available competing newspaper, thus decreasing company profits.

STORY QUOTAS

Story quotas can also be traced to economic considerations. A fixed amount of news stories each day is needed to fill white space in the newspaper. This keeps up the appearance that newspapers exist to present news, even though the bulk of revenues result from advertising, not the number of newspapers sold.

Beyond this need to keep up appearances, a quota of news stories directly augments advertising revenues. The advertising department of the news organization takes ads from businesses for future issues of the paper. This means ads will be laid out in a blank newspaper before stories are written. Advertisements adjacent to news copy can be charged a higher rate than ads appearing next to other ads. Once the advertising department has sold a given quantity of the more expensive ads that are to be placed next to news stories, the editorial department of the organization is obliged to produce a certain amount of news stories. Thus, reporters and editors are working under a quota set by advertisements sold. By meeting this quota, the company can realize a higher revenue from ads than if the editorial department produced unpredictable amounts of news each day.

THE NEED FOR PRESCHEDULED AND PREFORMULATED EVENTS

The newsworker's preference for prescheduled events (e.g., governmental meetings, press conferences, courtroom trials) and for preformulated accounts of events (e.g., arrest records, State Department press releases) is also a result of economic factors. Story quotas vary from day to day according to the amounts of advertising space sold. This variation is somewhat predictable. Bagdikian (1971: 97) points out that the amount of advertising in newspapers and, thus, the amount of news accompanying ads is based on

. . . when American families plan their weekly shopping. Those are the days when department stores, used-car dealers and supermarkets do their maximum advertising. Since quantity of advertising determines quantity of news, there is a minimum news space on Saturdays, Mondays, and Tuesdays, and maximum space on Wednesdays, Thursdays and Fridays.

. . . Mechanical departments producing a twenty-four-page paper, as they might on a Saturday, reserve their last hour for the few pages, like page one, that are prime news display spaces and receive news until the last minute. When the same staff put out a ninety-six-page paper, as they might on a Thursday, they require the same time for these last late-news pages. So they must work even faster in the early hours of the publishing cycle to process the larger number of total pages. On such a day, the gatekeeper [news editor] must send out masses of news very early in the editing cycle, to fill up the added pages. Very early stories tend to have no time relevance and often no other kind except that they are available and fill space.

Bagdikian is describing the effects of increased news quotas on editors, but the same could be said of reporters. In anticipation of a heavy work load, reporters will fill their quotas for news with easily available preformulated accounts that can be quickly rewritten as news stories. And if reporters are going to go to the trouble of covering an event that has not yet been formulated for them in a press release or a government report, then they will only want to cover something that is sure to happen, and happen on time (i.e., a prescheduled event).

Thus, as story quotas increase while the labor force and the time to fill these quotas remain constant, workers turn to reporting preformulated and prescheduled events in anticipation of a speed-up of their production line.

The implication of this is very important: simply by speeding up the production line the ideological character of news can be guaranteed. Without the time or resources to do any investigative work, reporters have less latitude than ever to follow up on their doubts of any given version of what happened and are more likely than ever to rely on factually safe, easily accessible bureaucratic accounts. Thus, without recourse to news policy (Breed 1955) or direct editorial intervention, news content can be manipulated indirectly through the pacing of the production process.

Paulson (1974: 9–10) suggests that manipulation occurred on a specific beat in which labor news was covered for a large Canadian daily.

A look at the formal organizational arrangements for labor reporting reveals important constraints on the reporter in the final determination of which raw data become a news event. In the first place, there are only two labor reporters (a day and a night one); this might be compared to the reporters who cover business, which number five full-time day people. . . .

Another constraint is the time limitations on the day reporter . . . with deadlines occurring at 7:40 a.m., 11:55 a.m., and 2:10 p.m. Because of the load involved and these time constraints it is difficult for a reporter to leave the desk to go "out on a job."

This not only implies that selective manipulation of the pace of production can occur on individual beats, but also that the production line can be speeded up in at least two ways: by increasing story quotas or by understaffing beats.

If story quotas were the only control over the pace of news production, then, following Bagdikian, it would be at least possible that on some days of the week (Saturdays, Mondays, and Tuesdays) the pace of production would be slow enough to enable reporters to do investigative work. At these times they would not need to rely so heavily on bureaucratically preformulated accounts and pre-scheduled events. This does not appear to be the case, however, because it does not take into account the issue of understaffing.

My own observations and those of other researchers (Epstein 1973; Tuchman 1972; Altheide 1976) indicate that newsworkers operate under a continuous work overload. Every reporter I observed had an indefinite backlog of stories underway and potential stories to be covered. Tuchman observed this at both a newspaper and a television newsroom.

. . . [T]here is always too much work to be done. In news work, no matter how many reporters from any one news organization may be assigned to a legislature or to work at a specific beat or bureau, newsmen (and news organizations) are inundated with more work than they can do. There are so many bills being introduced, so many committee hearings, so many minute yet possibly important readjustments in the distribution of power. . . . More important, the news desk, the beat reporters, and the news bureaus are increasingly inundated by larger and larger batches of news releases (1972: 123–124).

Although Paulson's study on the Canadian paper suggests that the understaffing of a specific beat may be politically motivated, the fact remains that there is a general tendency for all newsrooms to have too few staffers trying to cover too much news, whatever the topic of coverage.[8]

Epstein's (1973) data from the three major national television networks (CBS, NBC, and ABC) show that understaffing has its roots in economic considerations. Epstein points out that from an economic perspective it does not make "sense for a network to maintain anything more than the minimum number of camera crews necessary to fill the available news programming time" (p. 100). In television this is the case because

the costs for gathering and producing news programming is controlled mainly by the deployment of camera crews and correspondents. . . . [T]he number of crews deployed is expected by network executives to be related to the number of hours of programming rather than the number of possible news events (p. 101).

Epstein goes on to show that these economic considerations lead network news directors and editors to seek out prescheduled and preformulated events[9]—something we have already seen in the print media.

There is no reason to believe the situation Epstein describes is very different in the newspaper business: the size of a news staff is based on the amount of news space to be filled, not on the size of the community being covered, or on the amount of happenings journalists consider newsworthy. In other words, the overall economic logic of news reporting dictates the *minimization of labor costs* by understaffing the newsroom. This principle operates over and above specific managerial decisions to understaff certain beats, as in the case of Paulson's labor beat. From an economic point of view, it is a luxury to staff a newsroom with more reporters and editors than are necessary simply to fill available news space. A staff size based on other criteria, such as increased investigative reporting or broader coverage of the surrounding community, could only mean higher labor costs to fill the same amount of news space.

It is not so much that newspaper executives know for certain that an increase in staff size would have no long-run economic payoff in the form of an increase in readership. Rather, they have no way of knowing just what the effects would be. Changes in the quality of news coverage are not easily seen as the cause of changes in circulation (Sigal 1973: 10). Thus, newspaper managers have trouble justifying on economic grounds an increase in their reporting staff.

The Invisible Bureaucratic Subsidy of News

Reducing the size of a news staff beyond some point seemingly would affect the newspaper's appearance of providing good coverage. Where this minimal point lies, however, is uncertain because judgments of what constitutes good coverage vary widely within the news business. Nevertheless, whatever the management of a news organization has established as its minimal labor force in the newsroom, one thing is certain: this minimum is much smaller than what it would be if journalists could not rely on bureaucrats and officials outside the news organization to do much of their work for them. To understand the implications of this point, let us look at the nature of journalistic labor.

Unlike mechanical departments in newspapers where typesetting and printing have become increasingly automated, editorial departments remain labor-intensive. Although the editing of already written text can be partially automated through the use of computers, the work that goes into the construction of the written news story cannot be mechanized—at least in the foreseeable future. Newsworkers must have some way of seeing happenings in the world, interpreting what they mean, investigating them further, and organizing what is found into a coherent story. All this still requires a good deal of human work, i.e., wage labor.

As pointed out earlier, reporters do not do all this work from scratch. Indeed, routine news stories involve very little journalistic effort compared to the work done on occasional think pieces and enterprise stories. In routine newswork the detection, interpretation, investigation, and a good deal of the formulation of the written story have already been done by police, city clerks, insurance adjusters, morticians, and the like. And, of course, the work of these outsiders costs the news organization nothing other than the reporter's time to collect what is available.

Imagine the labor costs to a news organization if it did not have such bureaucracies to rely on for this essential work. The organization simply could not cover the scope of news it is accustomed to presenting without a massive increase in labor costs. In effect, an enormous network of governmental agencies, corporate bureaucracies, and community organizations underwrite the costs of news production. The modern news organization is predicated on this invisible subsidy.

Under inflexible deadlines and expectable increases in story quotas, reporters and editors cannot resist the preformed, prescheduled, and factually safe raw materials that bureaucracies provide. By propping up advertising revenues and at the same time holding down labor costs, news organizations create the work conditions which necessitate a reliance on the free services of agencies outside the newsroom.

From the individual worker's perspective, bureaucratic information is a practical necessity. From the organization's economic perspective, bureaucratic information is a welcomed subsidy.

The Politics of Newswork

This is not, however, the whole story. Reporters and managers of news enterprises are not the only ones welcoming the free services of the outsiders who provide raw materials for news. Those same outsiders—bureaucrats, politicians, press agents, and other routine sources—also welcome this arrangement. Their reasons, however, are different from those of reporters and publishers.

As every politician and terrorist knows, news has an instrumental value. To become a routine source for news is to have tremendous power in defining public knowledge of a world outside the individual's immediate experience. Thus, in exchange for free services, media organizations bestow on routine news sources equally valuable services: publicity and legitimation.

It is no surprise, then, that routine news sources are interested in cementing their bonds with news organizations. To the extent that sources recognize what they have to gain through their relationship with journalists, and that they act on this interest, they are what Molotch and Lester (1973, 1974) call "promoters of routine news."

News promoters are only too happy to offer their services to newsworkers. Indeed, knowing the nature of the newsworkers' bond to them, they have learned to cater to the practical concerns of journalists in order to guarantee that what they have to say is reported. Thus, politicians provide journalists with advance copies of speeches; press conferences are scheduled at convenient hours so that reporters may meet deadlines; press agents write news releases in story format; and special bureaucratic personnel—media contacts—are assigned the job of working with the journalists who cover their agencies.

All these promotional devices serve two ends: they are both tools for politicians, agency officials, or corporate executives, and they are conveniences for newsworkers. To varying degrees they all help the newsworker meet deadlines and story quotas; they provide accounts which, by journalistic standards, are factually safe; and they help solve a potentially recurring problem for reporters discussed in Chapter 2.

Recall that beat reporters operate under two environments of constraints: they must meet deadlines and story quotas established by their news organization, yet their stories are based on materials and activities which are not necessarily made available on a schedule compatible with the schedules and demands of their home newspaper. We saw how the beat round was structured to allow reporters to gear their work into both spheres. Now we can see that promotional devices, especially the media contact or the press agent, also bring these two spheres together for the reporter. It is the job of such an information officer to meet the journalist's scheduled needs with material that their beat agency has generated at its own pace. The media contact can deliver at the newsworker's convenience what reporters miss because they have to meet deadlines or because they do not have the time or resources to do investigative work.

Thus, news promotion is founded upon the practicalities of newswork. What ultimately leads the reporter to promoted news is not the guile of promoters but the lure of the promoter's agency which promises free, safe, easily available, predictable amounts of raw materials for news. Routine news promotion is successful insofar as promoters find ways to serve their own interests by way of serving newsworkers' needs. In short, news promoters put themselves in the path along which newsworkers are driven by the bureaucratic, normative, and economic logics of news reporting.

But to what extent is routine news promoted news? The question is not a simple one to answer because the distinction between a routine news source and a news promoter is often difficult to determine. The whole issue hinges on the matter of intentions.

Routine news promotion arises when someone in an agency recognizes the possibilities of making news by controlling what a reporter sees. For example, a police reporter may have snooped around a police department for some time, leafing through arrest and investigation records and badgering detectives for some interesting crimes. Up to this point, what the journalist makes into news does not appear to be something produced for the reporter. Rather, it seems to be produced in the normal course of police work. The point at which promotion is clear is when someone in the agency gladly delivers something to the reporter because they know "this will make us look good" or "make them look bad." What an agency may once have provided reporters as an afterthought is now provided with design.

However, news promotion also can exist when the reporter is relying on bureaucratic accounts which appear to have been produced in the normal course of agency work. That is, the mayor, the police chief, or the head of the vice squad may have ordered a crackdown on pornography precisely for the purpose of showing the public that something is being done about the problem. As Molotch and Lester (1974) point out, the conduct of agency work is routinely done with an eye toward how it will look to others, particularly the news media. News promotion may be so pervasive that the normal course of agency work involves the production of all publicly available accounts with an eye toward how it will look in the newspaper.

The problem for the researcher is that it is very difficult to determine in actual cases how large a consideration this is (relative to other considerations) for the actors in the reporter's beat territory. Until this can be resolved, it will be difficult to judge the promotional character of routine bureaucratic work and, thus, the extent to which routine news is promoted news.

Even though the extensiveness of news promotion remains an unanswered question, something important still can be said about the political interests served by routine news. Whether or not anyone consciously promotes it, routine news advances a definite interest: it legitimates the existing political order by disseminating bureaucratic idealizations of the world and by filtering out troublesome perceptions of events. The public is led to assume that the world outside their everyday experience is a proper sphere of official (bureaucratic) control; that everything falls within some agency's jurisdiction; that policy-makers do indeed make the important decisions while administrators merely implement those decisions; and that, with the exception of a few corrupt and incompetent officials, governmental institutions function according to rational legal standards.

Routine journalism communicates an ideological view of the world. What newsworkers end up reporting is not what actually happens, not what is actually experienced by participants or observers of news events. Instead, the journalist winds up weaving a story around hard data, which means the bureaucratic categories and bureaucratically defined events that agency officials mean to happen and need to happen.

Notes

1. News and Public Events

1. The description which follows is based on research reported in Fishman (1978, 1979). See these sources for a more complete analysis of the construction of crime waves and crime news.

2. The *New York Post* (May 9, 1977) cited this poll as showing that 60 percent of respondents felt assaults against the elderly had been increasing in their home areas. Moreover, 50 percent of elderly respondents to the poll said they were more uneasy on the streets than they had been one year earlier.

3. I discovered later that journalists in other news organizations had uncovered the same police statistics during the crime wave and had reacted in similar ways. Months after the crime wave, more complete police statistics indicated just what their initial figures had suggested, i.e., the rates of murder, robbery, and grand larceny against the elderly were on the decline when the wave of stories occurred.

4. The assignment editor started with these stories because his superior in the newsroom suggested they be covered.

5. Journalists' routine use of the news produced by other media organizations has been noted by several researchers. See, for example, Sigal (1973: 103), Epstein (1973: 150), and Cohen (1963: 54–65). Cohen was the first to point out the significance of shared news themes in his study of foreign affairs reporting.

6. In fact, the statistical picture of the situation varies, depending on how we measure the crime rate for the elderly. If we compute the rate as the proportion of elderly victimizations over all victimizations in New York City, then we find that the crimes most covered in the news (murder, robbery, and grand larceny) were all declining when the wave of publicity occurred. However, if we measure the rate in terms of the number of elderly victimizations per 1,000 senior citizens, then we get a mixed picture: murder and grand larceny were on the decline, but robbery was increasing. Ultimately, the issue of whether there was a behavioral crime wave hinges on our choice of which way to compute the rate. Both are reasonable. If we choose the method that shows an increase in the robbery rate, we have to decide whether the increase (up 3.4 percent over the previous six months) was large enough to warrant the term crime wave. There are no statistical rules for making these determinations; they are matters of interpretation.

7. Few criminologists would argue that police statistics are accurate reflections of actual amounts of crime. There is, however, controversy over just how inaccurate they are, i.e., whether they are of any value in inferring patterns of criminal activity. As this is not the place to rehearse these arguments, the reader is referred to two sources. Silberman (1978: 447–455) provides an up-to-date summary of the issue from the standpoint of one who believes

arrest data indicate the nature and extent of the crime problem. Hood and Sparks (1970: 11–45) survey the issue from the perspective of those who feel official figures and actual amounts of crime have an unknown relationship.

For years New York City police statistics have been suspect for a variety of reasons. At one point the FBI considered these rates so unreliable that they refused to include them in the Uniform Crime Reports (Silberman 1978: 449). After this event, the city's crime reporting system was centralized. As a result of this reorganization, in 1950 the recorded rates for several crimes jumped phenomenally, e.g., the robbery figure increased 400 percent (Wolfgang 1967: 33). In 1974 and 1975 another reorganization of department bureaus brought about a sharp decrease in the auto theft figure and an increase in the rape and burglary figures (Quinney and Wildeman 1977: 111–112). In 1966 the city police commissioner found exceptionally high percentages of recording error for certain crimes, e.g., only 22 percent of reported rapes were recorded properly (Hood and Sparks 1970: 37–38). In the mid-1970s a shift in the deployment of police caused crime rates to drop in traditionally high crime areas and to increase in the rest of the city (Quinney and Wildeman 1977: 111–112). Finally, there is reason to believe that politicians and police administrators intentionally manipulate the crime rate (Seidman and Couzens 1977).

8. For similar criticisms of these studies, see Tuchman (1978b: 56–57) and Chibnall (1975: 49–50).

9. I am indebted to the work of Dorothy Smith for her clear formulation of this point and for showing its relevance in sociological research.

10. To protect anonymity, all individuals and organizations in the "Purissima community" have been given pseudonyms. I am grateful to Kenneth Millar (better known by his own pseudonym, Ross MacDonald) for these fictional names.

11. These empirical studies are Tuchman (1969, 1972, 1973, 1978a), Lester (1975), Paulson (1974), Altheide (1976), White (1964), Gieber (1956, 1960, 1964), Gieber and Johnson (1961), Carter (1954, 1958), Breed (1955), Stark (1962), Sigal (1973), and Roshco (1975).

12. My original plan was to use Wieder's field notes for historical comparison. However, it turned out that the *Record* news organization and its reporters' practices had changed remarkably little in a decade. Thus, I used his field notes as an important supplement to my own observations.

2. Exposure to the Newsworld

1. The beat system of news coverage not only is typical of small newspapers like the Purissima *Record* but also is dominant on large prestigious dailies like the Washington *Post* and *New York Times* (Sigal 1973: 119–130). However, the situation is more complex in broadcast journalism. Few television journalists seem to work from beats in the sense that print journal-

ists do (Epstein 1973: 135–138). This does not mean, however, that in broadcast journalism most occurrences are detected and interpreted by reporters working on general assignment. Both network and local television news organizations heavily depend on the print media for their sense of newsworthy events (Epstein 1973: 141–143; Fishman 1978). Thus, newspaper and wire service reporters, who largely work beats, indirectly determine what most of the newsworthy events are for television journalists.

2. Purissima's alternative newspaper did not utilize beats and prided itself upon that fact. But as the paper began to expand its local coverage its staff debated whether beats should be instituted. Interestingly, it was decided they should not be used precisely on the grounds that to do so would cause the newspaper to shift from its distinctive "alternative" character.

3. During my period of study, the police reporter cited for me a striking example of this inappropriateness. The reporter's predecessor on the beat was caught sleeping with a police officer on the beat. The next day the reporter was abruptly transferred to general assignment reporting.

4. The phenomenon of jurisdictional ambiguity and the conflict it can induce within news organizations are discussed in Tuchman (1978a: 25–31) and Sigal (1973: 21–23). Also see Crouse (1974: 114, 260–261).

5. Boorstin (1961) accuses journalists of just this sort of illogical and corrupt practice after pointing out how modern news reports often precede the events they pretend to report.

6. The only exception here, if it could be called an exception, occurred when a reporter was temporarily assigned to cover a "special" story, i.e., one which was seen by the reporter and the city editor as outside the reporter's usual beat territory. This released the reporter from writing stories about the beat but not from the general obligation to produce written copy on a daily basis.

In a few cases, especially on very large metropolitan dailies (notably, the New York Times, the Washington Post, and the Los Angeles Times), beat reporters may be released by special editorial dispensation from the obligation to write every day in order to increase their investigative efforts on the beat. But these cases are rare.

7. I say "usually" here because some phenomena in the newsworld, i.e., press conferences, are scheduled around the constraints of the news organization (such as story deadlines). However, my data show that on the Record beat reporters encountered few such conveniences in their routine coverage work.

8. Although the round is rarely if ever noted in descriptions and discussions of beat work by social scientists and journalists, there is little evidence to suggest that beats exist without a routine round of activities. Whenever the routine aspects of beat work are described in detail (especially by journalists themselves), it soon becomes clear that a round is involved. For example, see Lincoln Steffens' autobiographical description of the police beat in New York City in the 1890s (Steffens 1931: 197–291).

9. Although this press room was set up by the sheriff's department for the

general use of all Purissima's media, only the *Record*'s justice reporter used it.

10. The amount of time devoted to a routine round of activities varies from beat to beat. While the county government reporter's round occupied eighty percent of the reporter's time, the city hall reporter's round took up somewhat less than half of the work week.

11. All rounds are not necessarily repetitive on a daily basis, like the justice reporter's round. Only some parts of the rounds of the city hall and county government beats are repeated day after day. Other parts of these two rounds would show up on the beat only on one particular day of the week or one particular day of the month. For example, the entire round of the county government beat changed from day to day but not from month to month. That is, while some of the required stopping points on the round were available for coverage every day (such as certain files in the county clerk's office), others were available only weekly, biweekly, or monthly (such as the various governmental bodies that met on different timetables).

Even though this complicates our picture of the round, it does not affect the essential point being made: the round is repetitive on a periodic basis, whether that period is counted in days, weeks, or months.

12. Certain other formally constituted agencies not mentioned in this list were included in the round of Wieder's justice reporter: the county welfare investigator's office, the police's juvenile bureau, and the city police commission. These, however, were included in his round on an occasional basis. Furthermore, when Wieder observed the justice beat in 1964 it regularly included the municipal courts. By 1974 this institution was visited only occasionally as part of the beat round.

13. In fact, to say that the justice reporter had no regular contact with these activities was an understatement. When I specifically questioned the justice reporter about whether he had ever visited the jails and prisons in the course of doing a story or had any contact with criminals, he said that he had not. Similarly, Wieder's field notes disclose a revealing exchange between Wieder and the justice reporter:

> I asked the reporter if he had any contacts with narcotics or marijuana users. I wondered whether or not he had these as sources of information for stories on narcotics use. He said that he had no such sources and that he had no contact with users. When I asked the reporter if he noticed that the evidence in police reports, that the public reads in his stories, permits his stories to formulate the environment of criminal activities for them, the reporter said that he certainly noticed this, and "The press is a vital arm of law enforcement in publicizing these things." (Wieder field notes 11-12-64, p. 4.)

14. Interestingly, the police reporter is engaged in a search for how best to collect information at the same time he is already collecting that information. This is a rather general characteristic of human problem solving,

whether the task at hand is compiling a list of fire damages, "passing" as a woman (Garfinkel 1967: 146–148), solving a word puzzle game (Fishman 1971), or doing a sociological study like this one. Especially when working on novel tasks, problem-solvers concertedly try to define the task situation (or determine the parameters of the problem) in the process of working the task.

15. Crouse (1974: 241–242) describes the White House beat in similar terms.

16. This phrase is taken from the programmatic statement of Benjamin Harris in his first issue of *Publick Occurances* (September 25, 1690), America's first newspaper: ". . . nothing shall be entered [in this newspaper], but what we have reason to believe is true, repairing to the best fountains of our information" (as quoted by J. M. Lee 1923: 10).

3. Seeing News Events

1. Although it is not very clear in this description, the actual plea bargaining session between the prosecuting attorney, the defense attorney, and the defendant takes place informally before the readiness and settlement hearing. The readiness and settlement hearing formalizes the already arranged plea bargain, i.e., the defendant enters a new plea and the judge signs a contract stating the exact terms of the bargain.

2. By a scheme of relevance, I simply mean a scheme of interpretation which is used for deciding the relative importance or relevance of various perceived and interpreted objects.

3. Not only did Slovekin fail to mention this, but the city editor, who also knew it was a case of plea bargaining, read and approved the story as written. It just did not seem to bother the city editor that the story did not inform readers of this fact. This is even more strange in view of the fact that one of the reasons the city editor wanted to run a story on Martha Mungan's guilty plea was *because* it was a negotiated plea (i.e., "Plea bargaining is a hot issue now").

4. There may be other factors which explain why negotiated pleas are rarely reported as such. For example, police reporters routinely have little knowledge about the actual plea bargaining process. They do not witness the negotiations involving the defendant, the defense attorney, and the prosecuting attorney, nor will they usually talk with these parties about the actual negotiations. But even this ignorance may be a product of the reporter's disinterest in anything but the disposition of cases, as the following interview segment between Slovekin and the researcher shows:

s: If I wanted to I might be able to sit in on some of 'em [plea bargaining sessions]. But I, you know, there's a limit, really, on how far you want to go.
MF: It would be fascinating, actually.
s: You know, not really. Just give and take. The guy'll say [the defending attorney], "Everyone else you've arrested this year on this charge you've

agreed to reduce the charge to such and such." I don't think it would turn out out be very interesting at all. It's just give and take. (Fishman interview 3-19-74, p. 9).

5. This distinction between hard and soft news differs from Tuchman's (1973). She claims that the distinguishing characteristic for journalists has to do with the scheduling aspect of the event. That is, an event which demands speedy coverage on the newsworker's part is hard news; an event which can be published at the newsworker's leisure is soft news.

I disagree with this distinction because events themselves cannot demand anything. Rather, it is the way journalists treat events that produces the sense of timeliness. Thus, Tuchman's distinction begs the question of how newsworkers know in the first place whether to treat something as demanding speed (i.e., whether to treat it as hard or soft news).

In contrast, I argue that journalists distinguish hard news from soft news on the basis of whether it is to be written from the angle of its phase structure disposition or from some other nonbureaucratically defined angle. The hardness and softness of news is not inherent in events themselves but rather in the decisions of newsworkers about how to cover and formulate occurrences.

6. The agenda itself institutionalized the distinction between important policy decisions to be debated and trivial administrative matters to be rubber-stamped. At the beginning of agendas there was a group of administrative matters—termed the "Consent Calendar" at city council meetings—which, as a matter of procedure, was to be quickly approved in a single vote. All policy matters were listed separately in the agenda and were debated and voted upon individually.

7. An experienced council-watcher familiar with *Record* reports of local government meetings could have guessed that a controversy preceded the vote on the basis of two clues in the story: (1) the kind of business reported was a routine matter, usually rubber-stamped, yet there was a split vote; and (2) that this kind of item was reported in the *Record* at all indicated something was going on, even if the reporter never explained why it was mentioned.

This reading between the lines is not farfetched, nor are the above clues useful only in hindsight. Some weeks after I told my wife about the street sweeper controversy and showed her its treatment in the *Record*, she pointed out to me in the newspaper a report of a piece of council business which appeared to have been treated in the same manner. She strongly suspected another invisible controversy, and, sure enough, on checking with people who had attended the council meeting, it turned out there was a long, bitter dispute over a routine agenda item of administrative business.

8. Kuhn (1962: 40, 59) has noted this same phenomenon of commitment to established methods (as he puts it, "preferred types of instrumentation") in the history of science.

9. This illegitimate quality of nonevents is closely related to Goffman's (1963) notion of "spoiled" social identity. Like the stigmatized person, the stigmatized event is shunned because it possesses attributes which are out of character with the setting in which it is found.

10. This terminology ("morally seen but professionally unnoticed") is patterned after Garfinkel's (1967) characterization of certain essential features in common discourse as seen but unnoticed in everyday settings.

4. Grounds for Investigating the News

1. For a particularly valuable historical account of the development of the ideal of objectivity in American journalism, see Schudson (1978).

2. For historical accounts of the emergence of the distinction between straight and interpretive reporting in the American media see Roshco (1975: 39–57) and Schudson (1978: 145–149).

3. The contrast between the investigative methods of reporters and those of police is clear in the investigations which ensued from reporter Jack Anderson's discovery of the Dita Beard memorandum. While Anderson authenticated his copy of the memo by getting Dita Beard and other principals in the case to *say* that the memo and its contents were authentic, the FBI authenticated the memo by running chemical tests on the paper and ink of Anderson's copy of the memo and then comparing these against ITT stationery and Dita Beard's typewriter ribbon (Anderson 1973).

4. I am indebted to D. L. Wieder for this formulation of news facticity.

5. Copyright © 1975 by The New York Times Company. Reprinted by permission.

6. Roshco (1975: 50) makes a similar point: the social rank of the source is the primary criterion journalists use in assessing the news value of any statement offered to the press. But the reasons Roshco gives for this differ from what I will argue below.

Roshco (1975: 62) says that the press gravitates toward routine dependence upon individuals who rank highest in social hierarchies for two sets of reasons. First of all, their attitudes are influential and their acts are consequential for others (especially those below them in the hierarchy). Thus, the press seeks out sources of the highest rank because, presumably, most people want to know what authorities think and do. Second, Roshco states that those at the top are the most visible to others and have the greatest opportunity to observe others. Thus, officials and authorities are easy for journalists to find and are convenient repositories of knowledge.

While this resembles what I have been saying (and what I will argue), there is an important difference. Roshco is stating that high rank brings with it the opportunity to be seen and to see. I am stating not that this is invariably the case but that journalists invariably assume it is the case, and thus help make it so. The difference is crucial because it is the assumption of competence to know which perpetuates and enhances the visibility of the source and ultimately the source's influence. Journalists produce the visibility of sources at the same time that they rely on it. Journalists augment the influence of sources at the same time that they assume it.

7. The sense in which officials can "see" more of something than others may be meant quite literally, as is the case with fire lookouts during a forest fire or coast guard personnel during a rescue at sea. More generally, though, the special vantage point of officials means that certain agency personnel—especially "higher-ups" in the organization—know more about certain occurrences because they command information and communication resources from their positions in the organization. For example, the radio dispatcher at Purissima's police headquarters would be expected to know more than most people about recent illegal activities in the community, and the city's public works director would be expected to know more than most people about the progress of dredging operations at the municipal harbor.

8. Slovekin's investigative work here apparently is predicated on what Garfinkel (1956) describes as "denunciation work" in status degradation ceremonies. Interestingly, the reporter's investigation of criminal matters of this sort seems to require him to play two roles in the degradation ceremony, that of witness and that of denouncer. In the latter stages of his investigation, as he is beginning to formulate a news story, the reporter takes the role of denouncer by assembling fresh evidence to show news readers that the accused is "not as he appears to be but is otherwise and *in essence* of a lower species" (Garfinkel 1956: 420; see also Cromer 1978). But in the initial stages of the investigation, as he is learning about the case, the reporter acts as a witness to the degradation ceremony of the criminal justice system. His reading of the court records is informed by the denunciation work already done by police and judicial personnel. That is, the reporter comes to appreciate the denunciation when he learns to see the accused not only as guilty in this case but as the type of person who would do such things. Moreover, as witness, the reporter appreciates the degraded character of Hallman with reference to its opposite: the upright character of Hallman's accusers (the FBI agents and the probation officer). Not only does this allow Slovekin to see Hallman as the evil character in this whole affair, but it also enables the reporter to treat the testimony of the accusers as competent accounts for his news story.

5. Methods for Investigating and Formulating Stories

1. I use the term "see" throughout this discussion only for convenience. The term should be taken in more than just the visual sense. I mean it to include any way in which something is sensed: hearing, tasting, reading, smelling, inferring, divining, etc.

2. The fact-by-triangulation method is used by a variety of other kinds of investigators besides reporters: surveyors, crime detectives, anthropologists (see Albert 1964: 54), and others.

3. Copyright © 1973 by the Washington *Post*.

6. The Practice and Politics of Newswork

1. See Garfinkel and Bittner's "Good Organizational Reasons for 'Bad' Clinical Records" in Garfinkel (1967: 186–207).

2. For an elaboration of this argument, see David Sallach's "Class Domination and Ideological Hegemony" (1974).

3. For example, see Chapter 4 for such a chain of accounts in the John Henry Truttwell story.

4. Notice that, within the bureaucratic logic of news organizations, news becomes just another input to the production process, like newsprint or ink.

5. This is undoubtedly why crime news is more frequent on weekends. The police never close. (See Altheide 1976: 70.)

6. This is simply an extension of the process of vertical integration whereby corporations seek to own or control everything from the extraction of raw materials to the marketing of finished products. While huge industrial concerns such as multinational oil companies typify this process, large newspaper corporations (e.g., Times-Mirror) already own forests, paper mills, truck fleets, and so forth.

7. Apparently some scandal sheets employ writers to make up a story of what happened based on a grisly photo of an automobile accident. Needless to say, these publications are not held in high repute by professional newsworkers.

8. The implicit perspective behind my notion of understaffing is a non-economic one: The newsroom is understaffed from a newsworker's perspective, not from the profit-minded executive's point of view.

9.

> Network news producers . . . have the problem of creating the illusion of truly national coverage, a world literally ringed with news cameras, and of "national stories," which are of interest everywhere, with the reality of a minimal number of film crews based in a few cities. To meet this demand, network producers have adopted the strategy of commissioning the national, or trend, stories they need well in advance of the actual happening . . . so that they can attain the maximum use out of the available camera crews (Epstein 1973: 103).

Although Epstein's data pertain to national network news, other studies indicate the same phenomenon of understaffing on local TV stations (Altheide 1976; Tuchman 1972, 1973) and in large daily newspapers (Sigal 1973: 10–11).

References

Albert, Ethel M.
1964   " 'Rhetoric', 'Logic', and 'Poetics' in Burundi: Culture Pattern-
        ing of Speech Behavior." In John Gumperz and Dell Hymes,
        eds., "The Ethnography of Communication." *American An-
        thropologist* 66 (December): 35–54.

Altheide, David
1976   *Creating Reality: How TV News Distorts Events.* Beverly Hills:
        Sage.

Anderson, Jack
1973   *The Anderson Papers.* New York: Random House.

Austin, J. L.
1971   "Performative-Constative." In J. R. Searle, ed., *The Philosophy
        of Language*, pp. 13–22. New York: Oxford University Press.
1961   *Philosophical Papers.* Edited by J. O. Urmson and G. L. War-
        nock. New York: Oxford University Press.

Bagdikian, Ben
1971   *The Information Machines.* New York: Harper & Row.

Becker, Howard S.
1967   "Whose Side Are We On?" *Social Problems* 14 (3): 239–247.

Berger, Peter, Berger, Brigette, and Kellner, Hansfried
1973   *The Homeless Mind: Modernization and Consciousness.* New
        York: Random House.

Bernstein, Carl, and Woodward, Bob
1974   *All the President's Men.* New York: Simon & Schuster.

Boorstin, Daniel
1961   *The Image: A Guide to Pseudo-Events in America.* New York:
        Harper & Row.

Breed, Warren
1955   "Social Control in the Newsroom." *Social Forces* 33: 326–335.

Carter, R.
1958   "Newspaper Gatekeepers and Their Sources of News." *Public
        Opinion Quarterly* 22: 133–144.
1954   "The Press and Public School Superintendents in California."
        Journalism Quarterly 31: 175–185.

Chibnall, Steve
1975　"The Crime Reporter: A Study in the Production of Commercial Knowledge." *Sociology* 9 (January): 49–66.

Cicourel, Aaron
1968　*The Social Organization of Juvenile Justice.* New York: Wiley.

Cohen, Bernard
1963　*The Press and Foreign Policy.* Princeton: Princeton University Press.

Cromer, Gerald
1978　"Character Assassination in the Press." In Charles Winick, ed., *Deviance and Mass Media*, pp. 225–241. Beverly Hills: Sage.

Crouse, Timothy
1974　*The Boys On The Bus.* New York: Ballantine.

Davis, F. James
1952　"Crime News in Colorado Newspapers." *American Journal of Sociology* 57 (January): 325–330.

Epstein, Edward
1973　*News From Nowhere.* New York: Random House.

Fishman, Mark
1979　"Police and the Construction of Crime News." Paper presented to the Society for the Study of Social Problems, Boston (August).
1978　"Crime Waves as Ideology." *Social Problems* 25 (June): 531–543.
1971　"In so far as the propositions. . . ." Master's thesis, University of California, Santa Barbara.

Garfinkel, Harold
1967　*Studies in Ethnomethodology.* Englewood Cliffs: Prentice-Hall.
1956　"Conditions of Successful Degradation Ceremonies." *American Journal of Sociology* 61 (January): 420–424.

Gieber, Walter
1964　"News Is What Newspapermen Make It." In L. A. Dexter and D. M. White, eds., *People, Society and Mass Communications.* New York: Free Press.
1960　"How the Gatekeepers View Civil Liberties News." *Journalism Quarterly* 37: 199–205.
1956　"Across the Desk: A Study of 16 Telegraph Editors." *Journalism Quarterly* 33 (Fall): 423–432.

Gieber, Walter, and Johnson, W.
1961　"The City Hall Beat." *Journalism Quarterly* 38: 289–297.

Goffman, Erving
1963   *Stigma.* Englewood Cliffs: Prentice-Hall.
1961   *Asylums.* Garden City: Doubleday.

Hood, Roger, and Sparks, Richard
1970   *Key Issues in Criminology.* New York: McGraw-Hill.

Hudson, Frederic
1873   *Journalism in the United States from 1690–1872.* New York: Harper & Bros.

Hume, Brit
1975   "Now It Can Be Told . . . Or Can It?" *More* 5 (April): 8–11.

Jones, E. T.
1976   "The Press as Metropolitan Editor." *Public Opinion Quarterly* 40 (2): 239–244.

Kuhn, Thomas S.
1962   *The Structure of Scientific Revolutions.* Chicago: University of Chicago Press.

Lang, Kurt, and Lang, Gladys Engel
1968   *Politics and Television.* New York: Quadrangle.
1953   "The Unique Perspective of Television." *American Sociological Review* 18 (February): 3–12.

Lee, J. M.
1923   *History of Journalism in America.* Boston: Houghton Mifflin.

Lester, Marilyn
1975   "News as a Practical Accomplishment." Ph.D. dissertation, University of California, Santa Barbara.

Matejko, Aleksander
1970   "Newspaper Staff as a Social System." In Jeremy Tunstall, ed., *Media Sociology*, pp. 168–180, 513–514. Urbana: University of Illinois Press.

Merton, Robert K.
1968   *Social Theory and Social Structure.* New York: Free Press.

Molotch, Harvey, and Lester, Marilyn
1974   "News as Purposive Behavior: The Strategic Use of Routine Events, Accidents, and Scandals." *American Sociological Review* 39 (February): 101–112.
1973   "Accidents, Scandals, and Routines: Resources for Insurgent Methodology." *The Insurgent Sociologist* 3 (Summer): 1–11.

Nunnally, J. C.
1961   *Popular Conceptions of Mental Illness.* New York: Holt, Rinehart & Winston.

Östgaard, Einar
1965   "Factors Influencing the Flow of News." *Journal of Peace Research* 2: 40–63.

Park, Robert E.
1940   "News as a Form of Knowledge." *American Journal of Sociology* 45 (March): 669–686.

Paulson, Marilee
1974   "The Ideological Use of Objectivity in Labor News." Paper presented to the Canadian Sociological and Anthropological Association, Victoria, British Columbia (February).

Pollner, Melvin
1970   "On the Foundations of Mundane Reasoning." Ph.D. dissertation, University of California, Santa Barbara.

Quinney, Richard, and Wildeman, John
1977   *The Problem of Crime.* Second Edition. New York: Harper & Row.

Robinson, Gertrude
1970   "Foreign News Selection Is Non-linear in Yugoslavia's Tanjug Agency." *Journalism Quarterly* 47: 340–351.

Roshco, Bernard
1975   *Newsmaking.* Chicago: University of Chicago Press.

Roshier, Bob
1973   "The Selection of Crime News in the Press." In S. Cohen and J. Young, eds., *The Manufacture of News*, pp. 28–39. Beverly Hills: Sage.

Roth, Julius
1963   *Timetables.* Indianapolis: Bobbs-Merrill.

Sallach, David
1974   "Class Domination and Ideological Hegemony." *The Sociological Quarterly* 15 (Winter): 38–50.

Scheff, Thomas
1966   *Being Mentally Ill: A Sociological Theory.* Chicago: Aldine.

Schudson, Michael
1978   *Discovering the News.* New York: Basic Books.

Seidman, David, and Couzens, Michael
1977 "Getting the Crime Rate Down." *Law and Society Review* 8: 457–493.

Sherizen, Sanford
1978 "Social Creation of Crime News: All the News Fitted to Print." In Charles Winick, ed., *Deviance and Mass Media*, pp. 203–224. Beverly Hills: Sage.

Sigal, Leon V.
1973 *Reporters and Officials.* Lexington, Mass.: D. C. Heath.

Sigelman, Lee
1973 "Reporting the News: An Organizational Analysis." *American Journal of Sociology* 79 (July): 132–151.

Silberman, Charles
1978 *Criminal Violence, Criminal Justice.* New York: Random House.

Smith, Dorothy
1973 "The Social Construction of Documentary Reality." Paper presented to the Canadian Sociological and Anthropological Association. Queens University, Kingston, Ontario (May).
1972 "The Ideological Practice of Sociology." Unpublished paper, Department of Sociology, University of British Columbia.

Stark, Rodney
1962 "Policy and the Pros: An Organizational Analysis of a Metropolitan Newspaper." *Berkeley Journal of Sociology* 7: 11–31.

Steffens, Lincoln
1931 *The Autobiography of Lincoln Steffens.* New York: Harcourt Brace.

Thomas, W. I.
1928 *The Child in America.* New York: Knopf.

Tuchman, Gaye
1978a *Making News: A Study in the Construction of Reality.* New York: Free Press.
1978b "Television News and the Metaphor of Myth." *Studies in the Anthropology of Visual Communication* 5 (Fall): 56–62.
1973 "Making News by Doing Work: Routinizing the Unexpected." *American Journal of Sociology* 79 (July): 110–131.
1972 "Objectivity as Strategic Ritual." *American Journal of Sociology* 77 (January): 660–679.
1969 "News, the Newsman's Reality." Ph.D. dissertation, Brandeis University.

Warner, Malcolm
1970 "Decision Making in Network Television News." In Jeremy Tunstall, ed., *Media Sociology*, pp. 158–167. Urbana: University of Illinois Press.
1971 "Organizational Context and Control of Policy in the Television Newsroom." *British Journal of Sociology* 12 (September): 283–294.

Weber, Max
1947 *The Theory of Social and Economic Organization.* New York: Oxford University Press.

White, David M.
1964 "The Gatekeeper: A Case Study in the Selection of News." In L. A. Dexter and D. M. White, eds., *People, Society and Mass Communications*, pp. 160–172. New York: Free Press.

Wieder, D. L.
1974 *Language and Social Reality: The Case of Telling the Convict Code.* The Hague: Mouton.

Wolfgang, Marvin
1967 *Crimes of Violence.* A supporting document submitted to the President's Commission on Law Enforcement and Administration of Justice.

Zimmerman, Don H.
1974 "Fact as a Practical Accomplishment." In Roy Turner, ed., *Ethnomethodology*, pp. 128–143. Middlesex: Penguin.

Zimmerman, Don H., and Pollner, Melvin
1970 "The Everyday World as a Phenomenon." In Jack Douglas, ed., *Understanding Everyday Life*, pp. 80–103. Chicago: Aldine.

Index

ABC, 149. *See also* Broadcast journalism; Network news
Accounts, 3–4, 55–56, 85–88, 107
  and the construction of reality, 3–4, 56, 96–101, 138, 164
  and phase structures, 55–56
  and societal self-knowledge, 3
  as performatives, 96–100
  bureaucratic accounts, 85–88, 92–101, 103–104, 107, 115, 136–138, 141–143, 149
  conflicting accounts, 116–118, 125, 130, 132–133
  credibility of, 98–101, 103–105, 107, 116, 118–120
  incompetent accounts, 118–120
  interested accounts, 123–131
  interlocking accounts, 87
  irregularities in, 109–111, 134
  levels of, 141–142, 165
  positional accounts, 120–123, 130–131
  treated as plain fact, 3, 85–88, 92, 94, 96–101, 134, 136
Advertising, 147, 152
Albert, Carl, 119
Albert, Ethel M., 164
Alternative newspapers, 27, 159
Altheide, David, 149, 158, 165
Andelman, David A., 93
Anderson, Jack, 163
Angles, 142, 162
Associated Press (AP), 90–91. *See also* Wire services
Austin, J. L., 96–97
Automation, 151

Bagdikian, Ben, 147–148, 149
Beard, Dita, 163
Beat, 16, 25, 27–30, 33–34, 36–37, 115, 145, 148–149, 153, 158, 159. *See also* City hall beat; County government beat; Police beat
  as an office, 28
  as a set of topics, 29–30, 47, 83
  as a social setting, 30
  as a territory, 28, 29–30, 33, 43–44, 47, 83
  bureaucratic organization of, 36–37, 41, 44–53, 74–76, 83–84, 153
  definition of, 28–30
  historical development of, 47–49
  overlapping beats, 29, 159
  rounds, 25, 33, 37–52, 54, 62–63, 142, 145, 153, 159, 160
  understaffing beats, 149–150, 165
Becker, Howard, 94
Berger, Brigette, 93
Berger, Peter, 93
Bernstein, Carl, 128–129
Bias, 118, 121, 123–124, 130. *See also* Fact; News bias; Objectivity; Selective Perception
Bittner, Egon, 165
Boorstin, Daniel, 12, 159
Breed, Warren, 13, 148, 158
Broadcast journalism, 158–159. *See also* Network news
Bureaucracy, 28, 52, 58, 62–63, 136–138, 141–143. *See also* Officials
  news organizations as, 28, 143–144
Bureaucratic affinity, 143
Bureaucratic logic of news reporting, 141–144, 145, 153, 165. *See also* Economic logic of news reporting; Normative logic of news reporting

Division of labor, 72, 145
  moral division of labor, 145
  political division of labor, 72
Durkheim, Emile, 100

Economic logic of news reporting,
    146–152, 153. *See also*
    Bureaucratic logic of news
    reporting; Normative logic of
    news reporting; Vertical
    integration
Editorial policy, 84, 89, 91–92,
    140, 148
Editorials, 70–71
Enterprise stories, 142–143, 151.
    See also Interpretive journal-
    ism; News analysis
Environment beat, 51
Epstein, Edward J., 149–150,
    157, 159, 165
Ethnomethodology, 3–4, 30. *See
    also* Reflexivity

Fact, 116, 144–145. *See also*
    Credibility; Hard news; In-
    vestigation; Objectivity
  and accounts, 92, 96–101,
    103–104, 116, 120–121,
    123–125, 130, 134, 137–
    138, 144–145
  and bureaucratic accounts, 85–
    88, 92, 94–100, 103, 105,
    108
  journalistic standards of, 17,
    92–93, 96, 136, 144–145,
    153
  societal standards of, 99–100
Fact-by-triangulation, 120–125,
    130–133, 164
  application of, 131–133
  prerequisites for, 130
FBI, 104, 105, 109, 158, 163,
    164. *See also* Police
  Uniform Crime Reports, 158

Feature stories, 70–71. *See also*
    Soft news
Filling in, 111–113, 114–116
Fishman, Mark, 157, 159, 161
Followup news, 66, 69

Garfinkel, Harold, 4, 42, 161,
    163, 164, 165
Gatekeepers, journalists as, 13,
    147
General assignment reporting, 24,
    27, 159
Gieber, Walter, 13, 77, 158
Goffman, Erving, 61, 137, 163
Greenway, H. D. S., 122

Hard news, 71–72, 87–88, 92, 94,
    140, 162. *See also* Fact;
    Straight reporting
  as bureaucratic accounts, 87–
    88, 94, 99, 140
  versus soft news, 72, 162
Harris, Benjamin, 161
Harris poll, 5, 157
Hierarchies of credibility, 94, 139.
    See also Credibility
Hood, Roger, 158
Hudson, Frederic, 90
Hume, Brit, 119
Humphrey, Hubert, 91

Idealization, 42–43, 62–63, 134–
    136, 154. *See also* Ideology
  of bureaucratic events, 62–63,
    134–136, 154–155
  of the round, 42–43, 63
Ideological hegemony, 139, 140
Ideology, 17–18, 32, 43, 134–
    140, 148, 154–155. *See also*
    Idealization; Legitimation
  definition of, 32, 134
  news ideology, 134–140, 148,
    154–155
  of the round, 43